The Revolutionary War

The Making of America- An Introduction to the People, the Ideas, And the Major Events of the American Revolution

By Jack Johnson

© **2016 WE CANT BEAT LLC**

Opening Scene

The Thursday of October 26, 1775 was a chilly day, but a day marked with clear blue skies and sunshine – an unusual sight for London, a city renowned for its foggy, dreary weather. But that Thursday afternoon, Londoners would not have mistaken the pleasant weather for any good omens. That Thursday, His Royal Majesty George the Third addressed the opening of Parliament on a distressing issue that gripped the island nation and had already claimed the lives of over a thousand young British soldiers – war with the American colony. American colonists were in open revolt against the Crown, but what was the proper reaction: war or reconciliation?

The king's royal cavalcade rode in splendor from St. James' Palace to the Palace of Westminster, departing at two o'clock and moving at walking pace. Almost six thousand Londoners had turned out to catch a glimpse of the royal procession and its gorgeous pageantry. The demonstration was certainly a sight worthy of the British Empire and the height of its power. The king's four-ton coach rattled the ground beneath its feet. It stretched twenty-four feet in length, and thirteen feet in height. Under its gilded crown were elaborate decorations that included three cherubs for England, Scotland, and Ireland, as well as four sea gods to remind all who saw that the seas belonged to the British Empire – an empire that stretched from the Americas and the Caribbean to India, an empire with one million souls in its capital city of London, the largest city in the world.

At thirty-seven years old, the king inside the carriage had decided that if the American colonies did not obey the Crown, then they would be made to obey. The fact that he had never been a soldier and had never actually visited the American colonies only reinforced his belief that the Empire's armed forces could quickly win a full-scale war against the band of American rebels who dared defy his authority. Lord Sandwich, the king's First Lord of the Admiralty, summed up his and the king's shared belief that the American rebels were "raw, undisciplined, cowardly men."

To fight these raw, undisciplined cowards, the king had already dispatched his three finest generals to the Americas: William Howe, Henry Clinton, and John Burgoyne. Specifically, he had dispatched them to the current hotspot of the fighting, the siege of Boston. And the king had practical concerns to worry about as well:

3

allowing the American colonies to fall would only embolden the Empire's other colonial possessions to break free as well. As he wrote to Prime Minister Lord North: "I am certain any other conduct but compelling obedience [from the American colonies] would be ruinous and...therefore no consideration could bring me to serve from the present path which I think myself duty-bound to follow."

Booming cannons saluted the king's arrival. After preforming his perfunctory welcoming formalities, he took his place on the throne, sitting at the forefront of the House of Lords. He went on to announce, in a powerful voice that carried throughout the House, one of the most important speeches ever delivered by an English king. He declared America to be in rebellion, and confirmed that he would meet that open revolt and "desperate conspiracy" against the Crown with an additional commitment of land and sea forces, including foreign mercenaries. Lastly, he denounced the leaders of the rebellion as seeking American independence, a claim that those leaders themselves had not yet declared. It was a claim that practically ruled out the option of reconciliation. If the American rebels sought independence, then it was not a tax-related rebellion at all, but an all-or-nothing struggle. A revolution.

After his twenty-minute address, the king returned to his palace "as peaceably as he went," confident that the Empire's immense naval and land power could stomp out this American revolution within weeks. The House of Lords agreed to the king's proposal for all-out war by a vote of 69 to 29. The House of Commons agreed to the king's proposal with even more enthusiasm, voting in favor by a margin of 278 to 108. The king soon thereafter appointed a new Secretary for the American Colonies, Lord George Germain, who declared that his mission would be to put down the "riotous rebels" in his new domain. How would he do so?

With a "decisive blow."

Table of Contents

Opening Scene 2

A Foreword from the Author 11

Section One: 1740s-1775, Sowing the Seeds of the Revolution 13

Chapter One: The French and Indian War... 13

Chapter Two: The Stamp Act........................ 15

Chapter Three: Benjamin Franklin and the British-American Tax Dispute...................... 18

Chapter Four: The British-American Tax Dispute Turns Violent in Boston 22

Chapter Five: The Gaspee Affair................... 25

Chapter Six: The Patriots Begin to Organize 29

Chapter Seven A: The Boston Tea Party....... 31

Chapter Seven B: The Patriots Mobilize the Militias 34

Chapter Eight: Prelude to the Revolution 37

Chapter Nine: The Conflict Goes Beyond the Point of No Return.................................... 40

Section Two: 1775-1776, A String of American Victories From Boston to New York City 45

Chapter Ten: The Shot Heard Round the World is Fired 45

Chapter Eleven: The Continental Army Rises.............. 48

Chapter Twelve: The Siege of Boston Intensifies 51

Chapter Thirteen: Benedict Arnold and the Early Victories 54

Chapter Fourteen: Benedict Arnold's Betrayal of the American Cause 57

Chapter Fifteen: The Battle of Bunker Hill.. 63

Chapter Sixteen: Colonial Victories Elsewhere in the British Colonies 66

Chapter Seventeen: The British Crown Puts its Foot Down on the American Rebellion...................... 68

Chapter Eighteen: Washington's Arrival 70

Chapter Nineteen: Washington Takes Charge........................... 73

Chapter Twenty: Boston Starves................. 76

Chapter Twenty-One: The Wait for Boston's Surrender is Over 78

Chapter Twenty-Two: Colonial Victories Elsewhere 81

Section Three: 1776-1777, American Victories Give Way to the British Empire's Might.................................... 83

Chapter Twenty-Three: The String of American Victories Begin to Falter 83

Chapter Twenty-Four: The Declaration
of Independence 86

Chapter Twenty-Five: The Declaration
of Independence is Revealed 91

Chapter Twenty-Six: The Setbacks Begin
and a New British Strategy Emerges.............93

Chapter Twenty-Seven: New York City
is Ablaze 95

Chapter Twenty-Eight: Comparing the
Armies.. 97

Chapter Twenty-Nine: The Fight for
New York City Stalls 99

Chapter Thirty: The Fight for New
York City Takes a Turn for the Worse 102

Chapter Thirty-One: The Long American
Retreat Begins.. 105

Chapter Thirty-Two: The Retreat Ends
and Washington Establishes His Spy
Network... 107

Chapter Thirty-Three: Logistics Start to
Cripple the American War Effort 112

Chapter Thirty-Four: Washington's
Launches into the Offensive 115

Chapter Thirty-Five: Commander Rall's
Fateful Decision at Trenton..........................118

Chapter Thirty-Six: The Aftermath of
Trenton and Princeton 121

Section Four: 1777-1781, Stalemate in the North and the Empire's Southern Campaign **123**

Chapter Thirty-Seven: 1777 and a New British Strategy 123

Chapter Thirty-Eight: The Battle of Saratoga and the End of Fighting in the North 126

Chapter Thirty-Nine: Bacterial Disaster at Valley Forge 129

Chapter Forty: A Very Deadly Winter Sets In 132

Chapter Forty-One: The Confidence in George Washington is Shaken 136

Chapter Forty-Two: Political Victories Roll In as the Military Fighting Pauses........ 141

Chapter Forty-Three: France Joins the War Effort..144

Chapter Forty-Four: Molly Pitcher 146

Chapter Forty-Five: The Northern Fighting Ends and the Southern Theater Opens Up 149

Chapter Forty-Six: The Meaning of "Patriot" Takes Shape................................... 151

Chapter Forty-Seven: The Southern Strategy Dries Up and Loses Steam 154

Chapter Forty-Eight: The Final Battle at Yorktown 156

Chapter Forty-Nine: "O' God, It Is All Over" 158

Section Five: 1781-1783, The Final Years and Aftermath 161

Chapter Fifty: The Pre-Negotiations Tension is Palpable 161

Chapter Fifty-One: The Treaty of Paris 164

Chapter Fifty-Two: The Post-War Continental Army and the Native Americans 167

Chapter Fifty-Three: The Meaning of the United States of America........................171

References 173

A Foreword from the Author

Millions of words have been spilled in discussions of the American Revolution. It might make you wonder, how do these thirty-five thousand words make any difference? The difference I hope to make is not a contribution to the world of American Revolution scholarship. Instead, the difference I hope to make is to introduce you to the American Revolution at breakneck speed. This book does not seek to add something new to our understanding of the Revolution, nor does it review the events from a perspective that has never been considered before. Instead, "The Making of America: An Introduction to the People, the Ideas, and the Major Events of the American Revolution" should be read as an easy-to-read reference point that contains from cover to cover *everything* you need to know about the American Revolution.

"The Making of America" is more than a recitation of events, however, and it is more than an encyclopedia. The goal here, as you could tell from the opening chapter, is to retell the story of the American Revolution in a way that captures your attention and is as educational as it is entertaining. This book covers the events of the American Revolution, but also their cultural and historical significance. This book also overviews the most important players on both sides of the conflict, and pays special attention to the key figures who led this military and political struggle and went on to found the American republic. Don't be fooled by the small size of this book; it may be small, but it is still packed with information that other books tend to forget. This book can and *should* be a valuable companion in any attempt to familiarize yourself with the people, events, stories, and ideas of the American Revolution.

Section One:
1740s-1775, Sowing the Seeds of the Revolution

Chapter One:
The French and Indian War

In the months, years, and decades that preceded King George III's speech, a series of sudden and violent events came in quick succession and turned the desire for open rebellion from a faint possibility into a probability – and then, lastly, into grim inevitability. But the American Revolution did not begin in a vacuum. Instead, there was a long, painful slide into the revolution. Historians often draw the beginning of the American Revolution back by well over a decade, concluding that, "It may be said as truly that the American Revolution was an aftermath of the Anglo-French conflict in the New World carried on between 1754 and 1763."

This North American conflict between the British American colonies and the New French colonies erupted as a small part of the worldwide Seven Years War between Great Britain and France. The "Anglo-French conflict" in the North

American theater is known by American historians as the "French and Indian War," in reference to the British Americans' two main enemies: the French military and their numerous indigenous allies. The French, by contrast, refer to this conflict as "La Guerre de la Conquête," or "War of the Conquest" – an important reminder of how even when we agree to facts, the different sides of a conflict can take starkly different views on what those facts mean.

The French and Indian War began over a dispute about who owned the Allegheny and Monongahela rivers in modern-day Ohio and Pennsylvania, and the first shots broke out when twenty-two-year-old Major George Washington and his militia ambushed a French patrol. Despite the fact that the two million residents of the British colonies vastly outnumbered the sixty thousand European settlers of the French colonies, it took nine years of disastrous British campaigns before France surrendered and had to reduce its Caribbean population to just two islands, cede its territory east of the Mississippi River to Great Britain, and cede French Louisiana west of the Mississippi River to Spain. Meanwhile, Spain's colony in Florida was lost to Great Britain.

Chapter Two:
The Stamp Act

On the world maps, Great Britain certainly seemed to emerge victorious from this conflict. However, the conflict had seriously drained Great Britain's treasury and nearly *doubled* Great Britain's national debt. Parliament sought to repay its newfound debts and replenish its treasury by imposing new taxes. Its Currency Act of 1764 restrained the use of paper money, which merchants had been using to evade debt payments. Its Sugar Act imposed extra duties on numerous products. When the British American colonies failed to raise revenue themselves, Parliament passed the Stamp Act of 1765 to impose the first direct taxes on the colonies, taxing all official documents: newspapers, pamphlets, and even decks of playing cards.

Thomas Hutchinson, governor of Massachusetts, strongly protested against the Stamp Act as soon as he heard of it, knowing that it was a terrible mistake. He spoke against it, wrote letters against it to English correspondents, and wrote a formal treatise opposing the act to England for circulation. George Washington, a bored military officer who had spent the past ten years fighting off Indian raids and leading reprisal raids against Indian forces, also thought that the Crown had made a serious mistake with the Stamp Act. This act, unlike its predecessors, was clearly just an unjustified attempt to take money right out of the colonials' pockets. The abrupt way that it was enacted and simply imposed on the colonials without any warnings or advance notice strongly suggested that the Crown and the King were ignoring the fact that British Americans had just as many rights as British citizens did under England's constitution.

Members of Parliament did not expect colonial resistance to Parliament's claim that the colonies ought to pay for the costs of their defense, especially when the taxes imposed seemed quite low. However, colonial resistance is exactly what resulted from these new taxes – immediate, spontaneous, and widespread colonial resistance. This resistance grew so severe that soldiers had to escort the Crown's tax collectors in colonial America.

The colonialists objected not on the grounds that the taxes were too high, but on the grounds that it was unfair for the Crown to impose taxes on subjects that had no voice in Parliament. In other words, "no taxation without representation." Benjamin Franklin (who had originally supported the Stamp Act, but quickly realized that this support was misplaced and would alienate his fellow British Americans) testified in Parliament in 1766 that British Americans disagreed with the idea that the colonies ought to pay for the costs of their defense. After all, the colonials themselves were the ones who had to bear the costs of the war with their blood and limbs, and the ones who had drained their own local treasuries to pay the twenty-five thousand soldiers who had bravely conquered France's North American colonies in the name of the British Empire. These new taxes were therefore a kind of double-dipping, in the sense that they forced the British Americans to pay for the war all over again.

Chapter Three:
Benjamin Franklin and the British-American Tax Dispute

Franklin is often identified as one of the seven key figures of the American Revolution, with the other figures being John Adams, John Jay, Alexander Hamilton, James Madison, Thomas Jefferson, and of course George Washington. Benjamin Franklin was born in Boston, Massachusetts on January 17, 1706, one of seventeen children. His father Josiah didn't have the money to send Ben off to clergy school, or even give Ben enough time to graduate Boston Latin School. Instead, Ben educated himself through voracious reading while he worked for his big brother, a printer. Because he was too young to be published in the local newspapers, Ben adopted in his submissions an older lady's pseudonym, "Mrs. Silence Dogood." His writings became the conversation around town. He wrote, for instance, "Without freedom of thought there can be no such thing as wisdom and no such thing as public liberty without freedom of speech."

Franklin loved books enough to ran away from his apprenticeship (thus becoming a fugitive in Boston), and went to the bigger city of

Philadelphia. There, he sought out work in print shops and printing houses. Books were rare and expensive at the time; he would have to work at printing houses and shops to have the best access to reading material. In 1731, Franklin decided to put his passion for books to good use by creating the first subscription library, an institution that pooled the funds of its members to buy books that they could all read. Franklin got to work creating the Library Company of Philadelphia, and hired the first American librarian, Louis Timothee in 1732. That same year, Franklin also published the first German language newspaper in the British Americas, *Die Philadelphische Zeitung*.

In his spare time, meanwhile, Franklin was busy inventing social conventions like the idea of "paying it forward," as well as scientific inventions, including the lightning rod, glass harmonica, Franklin stove, bifocal glasses, and the flexible urinary catheter. He refused to patent these inventions, because "... as we enjoy great advantages from the inventions of others, we should be glad of an opportunity to serve others by any invention of ours; and this we should do freely and generously." Because he was certainly not busy enough writing newspapers, creating the library system, and inventing various scientific innovations, Franklin also composed classical music and learned how to play the violin, the harp, and the guitar as well, while also becoming one of the first people who learned to play chess in the American colonies.

Politically, Franklin was rising through the ranks of public service in Philadelphia throughout the late 1740s and through the 1750s. He was selected as a councilman in 1748, then in June 1749 he became a Justice of the Peace for the City of Philadelphia. In 1751 he was elected to the Pennsylvania Assembly. Two years later, he was appointed deputy postmaster-general of British North America, and reformed the postal system so that mail started to be sent out on a weekly basis. The Pennsylvania Assembly sent him to London in 1757, and he stayed there for a number of years to further American politics, conduct more scientific experiments, then address Parliament on the question of its new tax laws.

Franklin's testimony did not convince Parliament to lift its new taxes, but he eloquently voiced the legal concerns that the Sons of Liberty were bringing to light, back in the British American colonies. They had formed the previous year, in 1765, and used public demonstrations, boycotts of British goods, threats of violence, and even violence to make their point that these new taxes were null and void, unenforceable because Parliament was not entitled to levy taxes without colonial approval. They formed a Stamp Act Congress in New York City in 1765, and drafted a Declaration of Rights and Grievances to formally complain that the taxes violated their rights as British citizens.

A new prime minister, Lord Rockingham, came to power in July of 1765. Under his leadership, Parliamentary figures began to backtrack from their argument that taxation did not require representation, and argue instead that the colonies were "virtually represented." When this proved unpersuasive and the British American violence worsened, Parliament finally repealed the Stamp Act on February 21, 1766, out of fear that the British Americans' anger was about to boil over into an all-out rebellion. Widespread celebration broke out among the British American colonies.

Chapter Four:
The British-American Tax Dispute Turns Violent in Boston

But the celebration would be short-lived. In 1767, Parliament's Townshend Acts brought back the Stamp Act in all but name by imposing extra duties on essential goods, such as tea. The distance of the Americas from Great Britain and the colonies' long, jagged coastline made it easy for merchants to avoid the taxes by sneaking past British authorities and delivering their products directly to American consumers. When the Townshend Act began, Britain therefore felt the need to step up its anti-smuggling campaign.

Under the Townshend Act, British forces in Boston seized John Hancock's sloop, *Liberty*, on suspicions of smuggling tea. Riots broke out in Boston. British custom officials fled. More British troops were brought in to restore control, but they were increasingly seen as a foreign army of occupation. Tensions simmered over the next two years, with colonialists (and much of the British public) feeling increasingly sympathetic to the Bostonian struggles, and with Parliament getting increasingly "tough on crime." In 1769, Parliament went so far as to reactivate the Treason Act 1543 and threaten to bring British

American agitators into England to try them for treason

The situation took a turn for the worse on March 5, 1770. A mob had gathered around a group of British soldiers, pelting them with snowballs and rocks. Despite an order to hold their fire, the panicked soldiers began shooting into the crowd, hitting eleven people and killing five in what would quickly become known as the Boston Massacre. John Adams defended the soldiers and helped them receive an acquittal for the massacre, but the Boston Massacre was a pivotal moment, one that permanently tarnished the British-American relationship. British Americans no longer saw the Crown as their own. The Crown had become something foreign – almost an enemy, even.

Parliament was sensitive to this development. Under a new prime minister, Lord North, Parliament went on to repeal all taxes but the tea tax. Cross-Atlantic relations eased, the boycotts ended, and only the most radical patriots like Samuel Adams (who was, ironically, cousins with John Adams) were still insisting that the tea tax was illegal, unenforceable, and a grave violation of the British Americans' inalienable right to self-governance.

Born to a religious Puritan family on October 30, 1735 in Quincy, Massachusetts, John Adams would graduate Harvard College in 1755 and go on to become the nation's first vice president, then second president. He is widely considered one of the key figures in the birth of the American republic. While his cousin Samuel sought violence, John decided to focus on justice in his defense of the British soldiers in Boston, then attended the Continental Congress as a delegate from Massachusetts. John was one of the early advocates for independence, and helped Thomas Jefferson draft the United States Declaration of Independence in 1776. Adams would then go on to negotiate the Treaty of Paris between Great Britain and the United States, ending the Revolution.

Chapter Five:
The Gaspee Affair

Two uneventful years passed, and British Americans who opposed the tea tax were largely ignored by a population of colonials who decided that it was not enough of a tax to make a fuss over. Parliament began to turn its focus elsewhere, figuring that the American question had been resolved decisively and amicably. Though the repeal of non-tea taxes appeased most of the patriots, tea continued to be taxed without colonial representation and in total disregard of colonial approval. The continued dispute over taxes made many British Americans start considering the question of their natural rights.

"Natural rights" referred to the idea in republican thought that all people have certain inalienable rights, bestowed upon them by the natural order of the world. Because people are born with these rights, not even the mightiest government like Great Britain could claim to take these rights away. Of course, it was not a popular opinion in Great Britain. John Locke expanded this idea of thought during his lifetime in the late 1600s (specifically, 1632-1704), and his ideas proved exceptionally influential on the founding of the United States of America. Indeed, his ideas about the social contract, natural rights, and the concept that people are "born free and equal" has brought many historians to refer to Locke as "the philosopher of the American Revolution."

One natural right that the tax issue and "taxation without representation" brought to light was the natural right of people to overthrow tyrants. If people are born free and equal, then it follows that the government has no right to impose its inherently restrictive laws without the public's consent. From that perspective, a tax without representation was no tax at all – or, at least not a tax that Great Britain had any right to enforce. And of course, many British Americans had to feel some concern over the "slippery slope" argument that even if these taxes were light, what laws would the Crown go on to pass if it had a free hand to pass laws without representation? What other burdens would Parliament impose on British America, without first seeking the colonials' approval?

On July 9, 1772, a group of Sons of Liberty members in Rhode Island decided to take action and remind the British Americans that the tax was a serious violation of their natural right to have a voice in how they should be governed.

They saw that a British ship had run aground in shallow water, and its crew was struggling to free their ship back into the deeper waters. The group of Sons of Liberty members recognized it as the *Gaspee,* a British customs schooner that sailed around in search of American tea smugglers to catch and imprison for evading the tea tax. It had been chasing after an American ship, the packet boat *Hannah*, when its crew brought it too close to shore.

Led by Abraham Whipple and John Brown, the group of Sons of Liberty members planned out an attack. The next morning, at the crack of dawn, they jumped onto their rowboats and rowed out to the *Gaspee*. They fought off the British tea tax enforcers, then boarded the ship, looted it, and set the symbol of the tea tax on fire. This event would quickly come to be known as the *Gaspee* Affair, and British forces took it very seriously. Interested in making an example of the Sons of Liberty, they investigated the arson as an act of treason, and hoped to ship back the arsonists to England, where they would be found guilty of treason and executed. Royal officials needed local support to find these Sons of Liberty, however, and that is something they did not have. The officials had to end their investigation without any suspects to ship off to England.

During the *Gaspee* investigation, Samuel Adams noticed that many British Americans, even the ones that were not bothered a great deal by the tea tax, disagreed with the idea that the Crown should be able to send treason suspects to England for trial. It was clearly unfair; a British jury would surely just convict whatever colonials came before it, regardless of how much evidence the prosecution put on. Colonials believed that for a trial to be fair, defendants had to have a jury of their peers – fellow colonials. Adams created a committee of correspondence in Boston, so that locals could discuss their opinions about the *Gaspee* investigation and formally object to their leaders about the idea of sending suspects back to England for trial. After the *Gaspee* investigation ended without any suspects, Adams kept his committee of correspondence running as a way to centralize the resistance movement to Great Britain's unfair policies in general.

Chapter Six:
The Patriots Begin to Organize

Other committees of correspondence spread through the thirteen colonies. These committees grew to include eight thousand individuals. Many of these patriots would go on to become the American Revolution's future leaders, such as Patrick Henry and Thomas Jefferson (both of whom served in the largest committee in Virginia, unsurprisingly the largest colony). These committees also helped form a new identity in the British Americas, that of the "patriot" (otherwise known as the "Rebel," "Revolutionary," "Continental," or "American Whig"). Patriots are individuals or members of a resistance movement who actively oppose enemy forces who are occupying their country. It is a powerful term, and it was selected by none other than Benjamin Franklin in a 1773 letter to serve as an umbrella term for the Sons of Liberty, as well as other British Americans who opposed Great Britain's new taxes. The committees of correspondence made a point of admitting entrance only to patriots. They also went to great lengths to exclude the group of British Americans who supported reconciliation with the Crown, identifying them interchangeably as "loyalists," "royalists," or "American tories." (For consistency's sake, this Book will refer to the opposing sides as Patriots and Loyalists).

As British American distrust of the British Crown grew, the patriots' ranks swelled. It certainly did not help matters when, in 1773, an unknown source leaked some very incendiary letters from Massachusetts Governor Thomas Hutchinson. Hutchinson argued in these letters that the British American colonists should not have all the rights that their English citizens enjoyed. This opinion confirmed many people's fears that their royal British leaders were conspiring to systematically take away American rights, one at a time, until they were second-class citizens in the British Empire. The Assembly of Massachusetts petitioned for his recall. Ultimately, Benjamin Franklin admitted that he was the one who had leaked the letters. Franklin had been the postmaster general for the colonies at this time, so he of course had come across these letters and decided it was something the world needed to know. Franklin, of course, was quickly fired by his British employers.

Chapter Seven A:
The Boston Tea Party

With astonishingly poor timing, Parliament at this time decided to pass the Tea Act, which gave England's East India Trading Company exclusive rights to sell their high-quality tea to the British American colonies, and which lowered the price of taxed tea that the East India Trading Company would sell to the colonies. A broad range of colonialists were infuriated: not only those who opposed taxation without representation (after all – the tea tax, though lowered, was still there), and not only the smugglers who would now have a harder time of smuggling tea, but also the colonials who feared that this was another step in the program to strip Americans of their rights, as well as colonial merchants who would be bypassed by the tea trade and lose their jobs. On December 16, 1773, a group of British Americans decided to take a stand by refusing to accept the latest shipment of new Tea Act tea. Samuel Adams led a group of Bostonians dressed as Native Americans onto the ships of the British East India Company and dump nearly a *million* dollars' worth of tea into the Boston Harbor.

Many colonials were alarmed by news of this raid in Boston. Even George Washington disapproved of the wastefulness involved in this protest, and the seemingly dishonorable way that the protestors hid their identity under Indian garb. A member of Virginia's House of Burgesses by this time, Washington suggested that the colonials ought to repay the Crown for the losses, thus distancing themselves from the hard-headed Sons of Liberty movement. However, Washington also agreed with the widespread feeling in the colonies that colonials ought to able to govern themselves and decide their own future, instead of being puppets to the Crown and its unpredictable whims.

Colonials for the most part supported this bold gesture, however. They would come to refer to it rather comically, as if to downplay its significance by referring to it as Boston's "Tea Party." Parliament was not so amused. Furious, Parliament acted fast in its punishment of Boston through a number of acts, altogether known as the Coercive Acts of 1774. These acts outraged British Americans, and cross-Atlantic relations returned to the earlier cycle of escalation that made the Boston Massacre an inevitability. Colonials like Washington, who supported the idea of self-governance but not the violent and wasteful display shown at the Boston

Tea Party, were now radicalized and just as furious as Parliament when Parliament punished Boston by practically imposing martial law and turning it into an armed camp.

Chapter Seven B:
The Patriots Mobilize the Militias

Massachusetts patriots formed a shadow government known as the Provincial Congress, and began training militiamen just outside of Boston. The committees of correspondence were also outraged by the acts they referred to as the Intolerable Acts. The committees therefore formed a provincial congress of their own in a meeting that fifty-six of their delegates attended in Philadelphia, known as the First Continental Congress. John Jay served as President of the Congress, and he is often referred to as a key figure in the establishment of the American republic. Born on December 12, 1745 into a wealthy New York City family, John attended King's College (later renamed Columbia University) and went into the practice of law.

In 1774, he joined New York's committee of correspondence as his first public role, and argued against the legality of Great Britain's tax laws. His contention was short and to the point: "Those who own the country ought to govern it." John took an unusual route into the patriots' camp, in the sense that he began as a moderate, and only then became more ardent. Most patriots began as zealous advocates of resistance, and only later moderated their views. His initial moderation served him well, as it encouraged New York to send him as their delegate, and encouraged the congress men to select him, the moderate, as their president.

Based on John Adams' proposal, the First Continental Congress imposed a total embargo on Great Britain, calling on all British Americans to avoid buying British products. This brought British imports to the British Americans down by a staggering ninety-seven percent. The First Continental Congress also threatened to stop all exports to Great Britain if its "Intolerable Acts" were not repealed by September. As serious and hostile as these decisions were, they were actually toned down from the alternative proposal from conservative Joseph Galloway, who wanted the Continental Congress to be a colonial parliament with the jurisdiction to accept or reject the British Parliament's acts. Instead of this revolutionary idea, the First Continental Congress agreed to obey Parliament and merely resist taxation without representation.

The First Continental Congress's bold demands went unmet. King George III and even Prime Minister Lord North believed that when push came to shove, Parliament stood supreme over all questions of authority in Great Britain and its colonies. The King wrote to North that at this point, there was no hope for North to recreate the kinds of reconciliation North had offered in earlier years to the British Americans, and that "blows must decide whether they are to be subject to this country or independent." Parliament therefore reacted to the First Continental Congress's demands with the Quebec Act of 1774, which expanded Canadian boundaries into British America. Parliament also decided to impose a serious restriction on British American merchants, declaring that British Americans could only trade with Britain.

But by this point, Parliament's words were not sparking much outrage in the British American colonies; their words were simply falling on deaf ears, and many colonials had simply stopped listening. The illusion of Parliamentary supremacy was over. The American patriots especially had grown tired of debating and letter-writing. They decided that the time had come to begin drilling militiamen who could fight at a minute's notice (thus the term, "minutemen"), and begin preparing for large-scale, organized violence. While they believed that the pen is mightier than the sword, they decided that when the pen fails, armed resistance as a last resort must take its place.

Chapter Eight:
Prelude to the Revolution

Two months after King George III's declaration that the British Americas were in state of rebellion, the American Revolution's first outbreaks of mass, organized violence erupted. Surprising no one, these first battles took place in Massachusetts, near Boston, at the cities of Lexington and Concord. With their goal of repelling the British ground forces, the patriots' militias served a new purpose now. But the militias were by no means new. Colonialist militias had been around as long as the colonies had been around, and were formed to defend local towns from Indian raids. By the mid-1700s provincial law required every town to form and properly arm militia companies of all males aged sixteen and older, with few exceptions to service. The militias gained valuable experience in conventional warfare during the nine-year French and Indian War, and had fought alongside British regulars.

On April 14, 1775, the governor of Massachusetts received orders from the British Secretary of State to disarm the Massachusetts militia and imprison its leaders. Adams and Hancock got out of Boston and fled to Lexington, a little town that stood between Boston and Concord. The Massachusetts militias had been stockpiling their weapons, gunpowder, and other supplies at Concord, which also housed the Provincial Congress. So, it came as no surprise that one day soon, hundreds of British regulars would march into Concord. The only question was when. Then, on the night of April 18, Paul Revere (and others) rode on horseback down this road to warn the leaders at Concord and especially the ones close-by at Lexington, "The British are coming!" Revere's other riders went out further, with Israel Bissell, a dispatcher of twenty-three years of age, going to New York and Philadelphia, covering three hundred and fifty miles in six days to spread the news of the revolution with the message, "To arms, to arms, the war has begun!"

In doing so, Revere's riders triggered the "alarm and muster" system that the patriots had developed decades before, as a response to the Indian raids. This early-warning system allowed the militias to assemble and prepare defensive positions while the seven hundred approaching British regulars were still well out of sight and blissfully unaware of the impending gunfight. The patriots had developed their system so well that even while the British regulars were still unloading their boats at Cambridge,

Massachusetts militias up to twenty-five miles away were already alerted to the approach and had begun assembling.

Chapter Nine:
The Conflict Goes Beyond the Point of No Return

Seven hundred British regulars stepped foot into Lexington the next day at sunrise. Their drummers were playing an upbeat little tune, an old folk tune that the soldiers had written some new words to, mocking the patriots. The tune was known as "Yankee Doodle Dandy," and the colonials knew it well. "Yankee Doodle" (also known as the "Lexington March") would become the Americans' first national song. One of the more memorable lines describes a Yankee coming into town on a pony instead of a horse, and throwing around Italian phrases like "macaroni" to describe his hat and sound intelligent: "Yankee Doodle went to town / Riding on a pony; / He stuck a feather in his hat, / And called it macaroni. / Yankee Doodle keep it up; / Yankee Doodle dandy, / Mind the music and the step, / And with the girls be handy." "Yankee" came from the Dutch pronunciation of "Johnny," a name they gave to the English residents around them. After the bloodshed around Lexington and Concord, the British would hear this tune again – this time, from the Americans' drummers, as they played the song back at the British and reviled in all its mockery.

At Lexington, the British found a surprising sight: eighty militiamen marched out of Buckman Tavern and assembled, with Captain John Parker leading them. It was tight-knit unit, with around a fourth of them related in some way to the captain. Between forty to a hundred spectators watched at the sidelines as the two bodies of soldiers stared each other down. The colonials were clearly outmatched by the regular force that stood at almost ten times their size, but the colonial force did not back down.

Captain Parker was not looking to recreate the Battle of Thermopylae, where a few hundred Greeks went on a suicide mission to hold off a force of tens or hundreds of thousands of Persians, and successfully bought Greece the time it needed to mount a strong defense. Instead, Captain Parker's instructions were clear: "Stand your ground; don't fire unless fired upon, but if they mean to have a war, let it begin here."

A British officer rode into the no-man's-land between the two armed forces, calling out, "Lay down your arms, you damned rebels!" None laid down their arms, and the nervous British regulars began to approach with their bayonets down. Then, a shot rang out. After the battle's smoke died down the fingers started pointing, with patriots accusing the British regulars of firing the first shot, British regulars accusing their officers, officers accusing the colonials, others accusing some unnamed person in the crowd of onlookers, and still others deciding that many shots were fired almost at once. To this day, it is a matter of speculation. This shot, in any event, is not the "shot heard round the world" that Ralph Waldo Emerson's "Concord Hymn" referred to in 1837. That shoot would be fired soon, however.

Whoever fired this first shot, both bodies of troops went on to fire a few volleys at one another, then a British bayonet charge dispersed the militia. Eight militiamen were killed by bullets or bayonets, and ten others were injured, including Prince Estabrook, a black slave who was serving in the militia. They managed to wound only one British regular. The militia at Concord quickly heard the news of violence at Lexington. A debate broke out as to whether they should remain at Concord and receive reinforcements from nearby militias or head out to fight the British on better terrain. A column of fighters marched out to meet the British at a ridge overlooking the town, then decided instead to march to a hill and watch the British while Concord was reinforced.

When the seven hundred British regulars marched into Concord, they were pleased to meet no resistance. They split up and searched for the supplies where their loyalist spies had told them the supplies were located. They also smashed the cannons they found at the town. Local residents at Concord also came forward to "help," wasting the regulars' time with misdirection and useless suggestions. One local resident decided to take a more direct approach with his resistance. Samuel Whittemore was seventy-eight years old and crippled, and he decided to go out with a bang. As the British approached his house, he grabbed hold of a rifle, two pistols, and a cavalry saber.

He took up a position behind a stone wall and gave off such accurate fire that the British assumed they were under a massive attack. They sent off an entire detachment to route him out. He continued resisting, killing about three British regulars and injuring several others. They charged at him, and he was ultimately shot or bayoneted in fourteen separate wounds. Later at the hospital, doctors looked him over and declared that the old man would die within hours. Instead, he lived on for another eighteen years, in time to see the British lose the Revolutionary War, the Constitution be ratified, and George Washington become president.

The Concord militia, reinforced by the militias of nearby towns, suddenly made its appearance. Four-hundred strong, they marched over to Concord from their hiding spot, and the hundred or so British regulars tasked with protecting that area decided to retreat. Neither side wanted to fire the first shot: the British, because they knew from the painful experience of the Boston Massacre that firing the first shot would radicalize the population; and the patriots, because their leaders wanted to maintain American innocence and make sure that the British would be clearly at fault for the next Boston Massacre. Little did they know that a series of unexpected events would unfold over the next few hours to create not only a massacre (of the British, this time), but a revolution.

Section Two:
1775-1776, A String of American Victories From Boston to New York City

Chapter Ten:
The Shot Heard Round the World is Fired

The cat-and-mouse maneuvering between the two bodies of troops, both unwilling to fire the first shot, left the British exhausted. They retreated to Concord. One of the fleeing British regulars fired a warning shot into the air. Two other regulars fired a shot as well, then a formed-up British unit at The North Bridge fired the first volley, killing two militiamen. *This* was Emerson's "shot heard round the world," and the feeling that this gunfire was heard across the globe would perfectly describe the shock that both bodies of troops were experiencing in that moment. Against all odds, and against their own plans, they were now firing at one another as if some kind of revolutionary war had just broken out.

As the two bodies of troops fired at one another, it became quickly apparent that it was the British who were outgunned and outmaneuvered this time. Panicked, the British regulars fled and even abandoned their wounded. The militiamen were shocked to see this, and decided to chase after the British. Nearby militias heard the unbelievable news of the retreat, and joined in on the chase. Moving more and more quickly to avoid being overwhelmed, the British retreated back to Boston, but made a deadly decision to go through Lexington. The Lexington militia, looking to avenge its honor and its losses, was eager to fight. Their volleys killed two British soldiers and wounded about six British soldiers, without receiving any deaths or injuries from the crestfallen British regulars.

The British regulars made it to Boston, their mission to capture the weapons and break the patriots' fighting spirit a total failure. By the next morning, fifteen thousand militiamen from all over New England had assembled around the city. Though the militiamen were referred to in some official documents as the Continental Army, there was no agreement on what the military force would be called in actual practice. Some referred to it as the New England army, or as the Army at Boston. When the Continental Congress appointed George Washington to take charge of the militia, the Congress referred to it as the "army of the United Colonies." Washington himself used a different term altogether, referring to it in his papers as the "Troops of the United Provinces of North America," and privately referred to the militiamen as merely the "raw materials" for a real army that would be created from it. The British and their loyalist friends still saw the "army" as merely a band of rebels, "a rabble in arms," "a preposterous parade," or "the country people" that did not deserve the title of "army."

Clearly, this was a patchwork collection of militias from all over – a patchwork that, in stark contrast to their counterparts in the British armed forces, could boast no flag, no uniform, no way of distinguishing generals from officers or officers from soldiers, no overall commander. Even their own officers had to admit that from a distance, they certainly appeared to just be a group of farmers who'd come straight from their fields. Nonetheless, the fifteen thousand soldiers laid siege to the seven thousand British soldiers currently in Boston, and the Revolutionary War had begun. Before, the soldiers and their commanders were Virginians, New Yorkers, Pennsylvanians, and so forth. By the end of the war, they would become simply Americans.

Chapter Eleven:
The Continental Army Rises

The militias besieging Boston quickly organized around one central militia, with Major General Artemas Ward (veteran of the French and Indian War) as their initial commander and the Provincial Congress as their ultimate source of authority. Inspired, patriots across New England also took action, starting to expel royal officials and royalist colonials from the colonies and take control of local townships on behalf of the Provincial Congress. Benjamin Franklin began convincing the colony leaders to join the revolution. He made his catchphrase, "Join or die." Franklin's tireless campaigning for colonial unity earned him the title of "the First American." His "join or die" attitude also echoed a March 23 speech that Patrick Henry made to the Virginia Convention, just weeks before the battles at Lexington and Concord. One line in particular from Henry's speech had spread like wildfire through the colonies: "Give me liberty, or give me death!"

At Boston, meanwhile, the militiamen had to come up with a plan. They had hoped that the British would come out of Boston and fight an uphill battle against the Americans, but no such attack was forthcoming. The Americans had no interest in storming into Boston, because most of the Americans simply lacked the "regularity and discipline" of a professional standing force. The majority of the militiamen were young kids who might follow an order, or, depending on their mood, might just walk off from their post without explanation, pick berries in the nearby woods, and come back to their post at some point later in the day. Having volunteered to fight for very little money (eight dollars a month in 18th century currency), they often considered it odd that there would be any fuss over rules and regulations. Even by the time George Washington was appointed to lead this army in July, his inspection of the young troops left him distressed at how inexperienced they were with the basic necessities of military life, including even "the absolute necessity of cleanliness."

Despite the fact that they were besieging the city, the Continental Army did not have even one trained engineer to call on for advice and planning. Further, the British had one crucial advantage: a navy. Because the colonials had no ships, let alone ships powerful enough to hold off the world's foremost naval fleet, Boston could be resupplied and reinforced with more troops by sea until the very end of time. Indeed, by the end of May, the British had already received hundreds of more battle-hardened troops, as well as three of the Empire's best generals.

Chapter Twelve:
The Siege of Boston Intensifies

The food shortage in Boston was actually quite severe, but colonial forces had no reason to believe that it would grow so severe (and worsen so much by the introduction of so many thousands more mouths to feed) as to force the British regulars to evacuate Boston en mass by March. Brigadier General Nathanael Greene, at thirty-three years old one of the youngest general officers in what constituted the American army (and, interestingly enough, with only six months of service under his belt at this time, he was also one of the army's newest soldiers), described the problem at Boston succinctly when he wrote:

I wish we had a large stock of [gun]powder that we might annoy the enemy wherever they make their appearance...but for want thereof we are obliged to remain idle spectators, for we cannot get at them and they are determined not to come to us."

Indeed, the Thirteen Colonies were not major producers of gunpowder. Even when Washington took control, he found to his alarm that the Americans had less than ten thousand pounds of gunpowder at hand, with very little gunpowder to be expected anytime soon. This report in particular stunned Washington so severely that he did not say a word to anyone for the next half hour.

So, the American militia decided upon a two-part strategy for kicking the British from Boston. First, the militia sent off on May 10 Colonel Arnold Benedict (who had not yet betrayed the American cause) and fifty men to capture Fort Ticonderoga's cannons, howitzers, and mortars, all of which the colonials had in short supply. In addition to the fort's long-ranged weapons that the patriots hoped to use in their siege of Boston, patriot leaders saw the fort's location as crucial. The fort was situated to look over a vital route between the Thirteen Colonies and Canada, and was also well-positioned to allow the garrison to attack the Boston besiegers from behind. Seeing the obvious desirability of this fort to the American cause, General Thomas Gage attempted to reinforce it as soon as he learned about the outbreak of violence around Lexington and Concord.

But the patriots had acted faster. Before Gage's order for reinforcements arrived to the fort on May 19, Colonel Arnold and about one hundred and sixty soldiers assembled near the fort at 11:30 at night, then rushed it en mass. The Americans had struck so suddenly and took the fort's British garrison by such surprise that only one person, an American, was wounded – and he was only lightly wounded. The sixty-eight defenders of the fort were all captured.

Chapter Thirteen:
Benedict Arnold and the Early Victories

Emboldened by the easy victory, the American forces went on to capture the nearby Crown Point in southern Quebec as well, again only suffering pnly one injury, an American who was captured by British forces. When Crown Point fell, another important position fell into American hands, as well as its stash of military supplies, long-range weapons, and the largest military vessel on Lake Chaplain. These lightning strike losses infuriated and terrified the nearby population in Quebec, which raised up a militia but did not get around to sending it off to recapture the fort. Fort Ticonderoga would go on to become the staging point for the American invasion of Canada, and its capture would go on to seriously interfere with the ability of the eastern wing of the British army to communicate with its Canadian wing. Connecticut sent over a thousand militiamen to hold down the fort while Colonel Arnold Benedict brought back the supplies and long-range weapons to Boston.

"Benedict Arnold" today is a reviled name, at least in the Americas. It is synonymous with treachery, betrayal, and cowardice. But his story is more complex than that, and perhaps the complexity only deepens the evil of his eventual betrayal. Arnold's story began no differently from the story one would expect of the average patriot. Arnold had been a British American businessman when the Stamp Act of 1765 seriously hurt mercantile trade in the colonies. Arnold joined in the chorus of voices in opposition to the act, and was one of the first British Americans who joined ranks with the Sons of Liberty. As a member of the Sons of Liberty, he was a die-hard patriot and was not opposed to use violence to oppose the implementation of controversial British policies in the Americas. He had even been convicted in criminal court on January 28, 1767 of disorderly conduct after beating up a loyalist suspected of ratting out Arnold for smuggling.

When he heard news of the Boston Massacre, he wrote, "Good God, are the Americans all asleep and tamely giving up their liberties, or are they all turned philosophers, that they don't take immediate vengeance on such miscreants." Then, the war broke out. Arnold was a militia captain, one of the first to arrive at Boston and begin its siege. He was the captain who had proposed to the Massachusetts Committee of Safety the idea of seizing Fort

Ticonderoga, which he had visited before and knew to be lightly defended.

Arnold would go on to rise through the ranks, to brigadier general. However, he was passed over for promotion in February, 1777 for the promotion to major general. George Washington himself stepped in, urging Congress to correct this mistake or risk losing a talented military officer. His plea fell on deaf ears, and he had to reject Arnold's request to resign from the armed services altogether. General Benedict Arnold did not see much action over the next few months as he was assigned to defend Rhode Island, and offered again to resign on July 11. He finally got to see action again, this time at the Battle of Saratoga, where his charges against British forces earned him some of the recognition he seemed to crave. He departed to Valley Forge and participated in the very first recorded Oath of Allegiance with his soldiers, declaring his undying loyalty to the United States and the American cause.

Chapter Fourteen:
Benedict Arnold's Betrayal of the American Cause

1778, however, would see General Arnold's loyalty come crashing and burning into the ground. General Nathanael Greene seemed to be the first to see the signs of Arnold's impending betrayal, having written on November 10, 1778, "I am told General Arnold is become very unpopular among you owing to his associating too much with the Tories." Greene received a disturbing letter from Arnold just a few days later, in which Arnold railed against the "deplorable" and "horrid" situation of the colonies, and seemed to believe that the American war was already at its end, with Congress ensnared in internal fighting and the country's currency depreciating into worthlessness. He predicted "impending ruin" of the American cause.

In May 1779, at around the time Thomas Jefferson left the Second Continental Congress to become Virginia's governor, Arnold met with a Joseph Stansbury, who then "went secretly to New York with a tender of [Arnold's] services to Sir Henry Clinton." Arnold would go on to sell American secrets to the British over the next year, starting that July by providing the British with information on American troop locations and strengths and the whereabouts of where the British could find American military supplies, all while constantly asking for more and more payment in exchange for the flow of information. His deceit and betrayal only worsened over time, especially when he decided that an alliance with France was a grave mistake for the new America. When he was entrusted with command at the West Point military academy, he systematically weakened its defenses and military defensive abilities. He failed to order supplies he needed to order, and drained the supplies that West Point already had at hand.

Arnold provided his British spy with information on how West Point could be captured, and this proved to be his undoing. The spy, Major John André, was captured by patriots, with the Arnold papers about capturing West Point on his person. As fate would have it, George Washington was visiting West Point on that day. Reports during the Revolution describe Washington as rarely riding at anything less that a full gallop, so one could imagine the terror sinking into Arnold's heart when he learned of André's capture. Washington was supposed to meet with Arnold at West Point's Robinson house, but instead he found Arnold missing and his chief staff aid in Arnold's place.

His chief staff aid was Alexander Hamilton. Hamilton at this time may have been a mere aid, but he would go on to become one of the seven key Founding Fathers, earning this position by establishing the nation's financial system. Born in the British West Indies at some point between 1755 and 1757, Hamilton was orphaned as a child. He graduated King's College (now Columbia University) with the generous support of some wealthy men who recognized his abilities and talent, then joined the militia as an artillery captain. Soon thereafter, he became Washington's senior aid, and Washington quickly came to rely on Hamilton to deliver important messages to generals. After the war, Hamilton would be elected to the Congress and would go on to found the Bank of New York, as well as the Federalist Party. When Washington became president, he brought Hamilton along with him as the first Secretary of the Treasury. Later in his life, in 1804, Hamilton would be challenged by Aaron Burr to a duel, as Burr had been offended at some of Hamilton's comments. That famous duel resulted in Hamilton being shot, and Hamilton died the next day of his wounds.

At the Robinson house, with Arnold's wife just a room away but unaware of her husband's treachery, Hamilton gave his commander in chief a handful of papers that were captured from André and explained Arnold's absence. The great war hero, Benedict Arnold, had tried to sell West Point to the British. Just an hour before Washington's arrival to West Point, Arnold had found out about André's capture and fled immediately – so suddenly, in fact, that he left his wife there without telling her of his departure. When she learned of the news, she broke into hysterics: shouting, tearing at her clothes, speaking in partial sentences, and generally thrashing about while Washington and his officers watched with alarm. Helpfully enough for her, Washington understood that she was not to blame for her husband's actions, she had not been part of Arnold's plot, and he made sure that the soldiers around him did not harm Ms. Arnold out of revenge.

Washington took the news calmly, as always. Some people had a love for America that no bayonet could pierce; others, he'd learned, did not hold onto such a steadfast loyalty. They were unable to "remove from the smoke of his own chimney," as Washington often described men who were all too sensitive to the realities of army life. He had been caught seriously off guard during the siege of Boston when a friend of his and the surgeon general of the army, Dr. Benjamin Church, betrayed the American cause by jumping ships onto Great Britain's side. Of course, the loss of a war hero like Arnold made him wonder who could be trusted, and reminded him that even his most senior officers and most experienced officers might defect at any moment. But since 1775, Washington had seen a number of men he'd trusted trade sides; to a large extent, he'd simply grown to accept the fact that some Americans would lose their valor and switch sides.

Acceptance of that likelihood did not mean tolerance of it, however. Under Washington's orders, American forces went on the hunt for the traitor, but Arnold escaped to a British vessel on the Hudson River. He became a brigadier general for the British, and led British regulars on numerous raids into Virginia, even capturing Richmond temporarily and torching it – thus earning his eternally notorious place in American lore. Calm as Washington tended to be, even in the face of infuriating setbacks and betrayals, he showed his inner anger at this incident when he made a point of trying to infiltrate spies into New York and capture Arnold. That plan had very nearly succeeded, too, with Arnold escaping through pure luck.

After the war, Arnold retired to London, was welcomed by King George III himself, and died in peace. Major André, by contrast, received the usual punishment given to spies in that time – within a week of his capture, he was executed.

Chapter Fifteen:
The Battle of Bunker Hill

In 1775, Benedict Arnold was still a colonel and a diehard patriot who was quickly rising through the rank and hauling back badly needed weapons for the siege of Boston. The second stage of the Boston siege plan was to put these captured canons and the colonialists' own cannons on the hills around Boston and fire at those ships, as well as at the British defensive positions in Boston. By mid-June, the artillery positions were set up and their defenses prepared. The British had been constantly watching through their tactical telescopes the action around the hills (as one trapped Bostonian wrote rather acidly, "It seemed to be the principle employment of both armies to look at each other with spyglasses."), but they had underestimated the problem of letting the patriots have the hills.

They fired on the work parties from time to time, and both sides staged occasional night raids. But for the most part, the Americans toiling with picks and shovels around the hillsides were left alone. When the first shots started flying into Boston Harbor and damaging Great Britain's precious ships, the British generals knew they had made a terrible miscalculation. After some debate, they sent over three thousand regulars up the hills, and were particularly focused on the most annoying cannons at Bunker Hill.

The British managed to capture the hills, but only after stiff resistance and a tremendous loss of British lives. Over one thousand British regulars were killed at what would become known as the Battle of Bunker Hill. Because officers tended to lead British charges, a disproportionate number of the wounded were officers, the most trained and experienced members of Great Britain's ground forces. A British general at Boston wrote in his diary that, "A few more such victories would have shortly put an end to British dominion in America." The colonialists, by contrast, lost about one hundred and forty men.

Though the British forces had recaptured the hill, their generals could hardly report it as a victory. George Washington was on his way to take charge of the militia around Boston (the Second Continental Congress appointed him on June 15, two days before the Battle of Bunker Hill, to become the commander in chief of all American forces) when he heard the news of Bunker Hill, and the news gave him his first ray of hope that this seemingly impossible war against the undisputed superpower of the 18th century might actually be won.

Chapter Sixteen:
Colonial Victories Elsewhere in the British Colonies

In November, five hundred and sixty patriots led by Major General Nathaniel Greene sparked the first outbreak of organized violence in the southern theater, in South Carolina, when they laid siege to the nearly two thousand South Carolina loyalists in the town of Ninety Six. Despite the loyalists' incredible superiority in terms of manpower, they chose to retreat after suffering four losses and twenty wounded men. Within a matter of days, patriot forces under Continental Army Brigadier General Richard Montgomery seized and took occupation of Montreal, Canada, without any resistance. Within weeks, on December 11, Virginia would also see its loyalist forces routed by patriots, who torched the important British shipping port of Norfolk.

Separated from the New World by three thousand miles of ocean, the English only received accounts of the American victories a month or more later. When the first news of Lexington and Concord reached London, it was already the end of May and Parliament had already begun its long summer holiday.

Announcements of Bunker Hill arrived in London at the end of July, marking a summer of dreary news. The English leadership struggled to contain the disgrace from the reports of the capture of Fort Ticonderoga, Crown Point, Ninety Six, Montreal, and Norfolk, and especially reports of the massive casualties from Bunker Hill.

The sheer number and magnitude of these setbacks forced Parliament, the King, and the military establishment to reconsider their dismissive beliefs about the colonial military capabilities. Lord North, for instance, began suggesting that the situation in American should no longer be considered as a rebellion, but as a "foreign war" that required the employment of "every expedient." He secretly began negotiations with several German princes, particularly in Hesse and Brunswick, to hire thousands of German mercenary troops. The English leadership begrudgingly recognized the patriots' army for what it was: not a large-scale riot of individuals, but an organized military force. Indeed, all but thirty units of the present-day United States Army can trace their creation back to this colonial army.

Chapter Seventeen:
The British Crown Puts its Foot Down on the American Rebellion

Humiliated, King George took swift action. Within days, he fired the British commander in chief at Boston, General Gage, and replaced him with General William Howe. The King declared that members of the Continental Congress were traitors – a serious declaration, because the penalty for treason was death. After a quick meeting at 10 Downing Street on July 26, the King and his Cabinet decided that they would sent two thousand British regulars to Boston as soon as possible, and to plant an army of no less than twenty thousand regulars by the time spring rolled around.

That winter, emboldened American forces decided to complement their siege of Boston by invading Great Britain's possession up north, Canada. They invaded from Fort Ticonderoga and Montreal, and firmly believed that the seemingly endless string of American victories would continue unabated. This expedition was led by Colonel Benedict Arnold, but it proved to be an overextension of the patriots' military might, however, and ended up with the expeditionary force largely dying of smallpox or getting captured by the end of December, 1775.

Chapter Eighteen:
Washington's Arrival

With colonial passions cooled after the failure in Canada, the first few months of 1776 were months of reorganization and consolidation. George Washington got to his post at Boston (which he had only been to once, briefly, as a young Virginia colonel who had arrived in the ultimately unsuccessful attempt of transitioning from the Virginian militia to a commission in the British army) and assumed command of the Continental Army on July 3, 1775. At this early point in the war, which was really still just a large protest against the Crown's and King's unfair treatment of British Americans, nobody would have guessed that one year and one day later, the Declaration of Independence for the newly formed United States of American would be signed.

Like Thomas Jefferson, Washington was a member of Virginia's House of Burgesses, and was sent to attend the First Continental Congress on behalf of the House. He played little role in the First Continental Congress, but found himself suddenly at the center of attention in the Second Continental Congress. Washington may have been far less educated than the Jeffersons and Benjamin Franklins in the room, but he had one thing they didn't: military experience. Unlike them, Washington had actually led men into battle against the French and Indians. Unlike anyone else in the room, Washington knew how the British army worked, how British soldiers fought, and how British officers thought because Washington had trained alongside them, and had nearly received a commission from the British army.

When the Second Continental Congress saw the violence escalating and began talking about the possibility of a prolonged war with the British Empire, Washington decided to toss aside his civilian politicians' clothes and wear his military uniform instead, reminding the politicians around him who he was and where he'd come from. By wearing his uniform during the congressional meetings, he had only intended to bolster his opinions as expert military opinions instead of the opinions he heard around him, vague opinions which were merely civilian speculations. But ultimately, his gestures convinced the men in the room to appoint him as the war effort's overall commander in chief.

Washington took up residence in one of the most elegant, largest houses in town, a

Georgian mansion that had belonged to a loyalist, John Vassall, who had taken what he'd expected to be refuge in Boston. One soldier described the incredible pomp and circumstance of Washington's arrival, saying: *"His excellency was on horseback, in company with several military gentlemen. It was not difficult to distinguish him from all others. He is tall and well-proportioned, and his personal appearance truly noble and majestic."*

Brigadier General Nathanael Greene recalled the moment of Washington's arrival as well: "Joy was visible on every countenance, and it seemed as if the spirit of conquest breathed through the whole army." "His Excellency" was certainly in the prime of his life at this point. He had mastered a commanding presence, and stood over his colleagues at six feet two inches tall. Despite decades of military service, his face was largely absent of wrinkles, though his sun-beaten face, like many soldiers' faces, was not without a few scars of smallpox. Despite the fanfare and near-worship that followed him around everything and practically granted him celebrity status (one observer said, "There is not a king in Europe that would not look like a *valet de chamber* by his [Washington's] side."), if not demi-god status, his character showed no hint of arrogance.

Chapter Nineteen:
Washington Takes Charge

As Washington himself had said to the Congressmen who had appointed him to be commander in chief: "I am truly sensible of the high honor done me in this appointment, yet I feel great distress from a consciousness that my abilities and military experience may not be equal to the extensive and important trust. However, as the Congress desire I[t], I will enter upon the momentous duty, and exert every power I possess in their service and for the support of the glorious Cause." Washington immediately found that it really would take every power he could summon to lead this Continental Army. It was hardly a fine-tuned instrument. He asked for an accounting from its previous commander, Artemas Ward. Despite this being a standard, simple request, the fact was that nobody knew just how many British Americans were in this army. It ended up taking a week to count all the heads, a feat that Washington had been able to do in hours when he was commanding Virginia's militia alongside the British regulars.

'Discipline" was also not a word that many men in this New England army were familiar with. The words he used to describe his soldiers were not flattering; they were "nasty," "dirty," and "raw" soldiers. Washington was in many ways appalled at the condition of his army. Still, he had a task to accomplish, and he would not shirk from it just because it was a difficult task. So, Washington quickly imposed some sense of regularity into the army. He began with the most important thing first, namely: the very problematic lack of a uniform. Washington could not find an overall uniform for his army, so he devised a clever alternative to a uniform garb. He instructed that major generals wear purple ribbons across their chests, that brigadier generals wear pink ribbons across their chests, that field officers wear cockades of certain colors in their hats, and that sergeants tie a red cloth tot heir right shoulders.

The second disciplinary measure Washington felt compelled to take was the court-martial process. He ordered the courts of military justice to open their doors and pass judgment on the worst cases of disobedience, especially from the officer corps. He decided this would be the most efficient way to drive out the weak and the cowards. By the end of December, over fifty officers had gone through the courts-martial process, with almost all of them being convicted of crimes that ranged from fraudulent handling of provisions, cowardice, profane swearing, beating a soldier, striking a superior officer, and neglect of duty.

Chapter Twenty:
Boston Starves

Aside from instilling a sense of law and order within the army's ranks, Washington had a primary objective as the commander in chief of the Continental Army: namely, to put an end to the siege of Boston. It was a formidable task, one that seemed to go on and on with little apparent progress because the British could indefinitely resupply themselves by sea. But the situation in Boston was in fact a dire situation. At the end of summer, a British ship sailed out of Boston and docked at Plymouth. A published account described the shocking appearance of the royal forces:

A few of the men came on shore, when never hardly were seen such objects: some without legs, and others without arms; and their clothes hanging on them like a loose morning gown, so much were they fallen away by sickness and want of nourishment. There were, moreover, near sixty women and children on board, the widows and children of men who were slain. Some of these too exhibited a most shocking spectacle; and even the vessel itself, though very large, was almost intolerable, from the stench arising from the sick and wounded.

Another royalist soldier in Boston described the situation before his eyes in the *General Evening Post*, writing that nothing but "melancholy, disease, and death" were in Boston. A British American stuck in Boston wrote to his half-brother on the outside that it was "inconceivable the Distress and Ruin this unnatural dispute has caused to this town and its inhabitants. Almost every shop and store is shut. No business of any kind going on. You will here wish to know how it is with me. I can only say that I am with the multitude rendered very unhappy; the little I had collected, entirely lost the Cloaths upon my back and a few Dollars in my pocket are now the only property which I have the least Command of. What is due to me I can't get and have now an hundred guineas worth of business begun which will never afford me an hundred farthings." It is no surprise, then, that the British generals in Boston were having a difficult time preventing their less motivated men from deserting the Crown altogether, and showing up to the American lines half-starved and disgruntled, eager to spill all the secrets they knew for a bit of bread.

Chapter Twenty-One:
The Wait for Boston's Surrender is Over

By mid-March, Washington had grown tired of the waiting game. The British were not about to evacuate Boston, however serious their struggles might be inside of the city. At the same time, however, Washington couldn't just summon up the gunpowder he needed for an assault. Instead, he came to an ingenious compromise between doing nothing and doing something: he decided that the Continental Army would have to *appear* to do something. Towards that end, he decided to send out all of his cannons at once. One morning, then, the British regulars woke up to see the hills bristling with cannon. A vicious attack seemed imminent. Seeing the hopelessness in their situation, the British generals quickly called for an all-out mass evacuation of Boston before the shelling began. During the Civil War, desperate Confederate generals found themselves in a similar situation, and took this kind of gamble even further by creating "Quaker Guns," which were just logs painted to look like artillery.

Washington later wrote to Congress, "To maintain a post within musket shot of the enemy for six months without powder...is more than probably ever was attempted" in the history of war. The truth was that the Americans had barely had enough gunpowder to fight off a British attack. This was the realization that led Washington to "not utter a word for half an hour," according to Brigadier General John Sullivan. Indeed, the colonials would have been able to fire off only a handful of volleys before retreating. But the British were so humbled by Bunker Hill that their generals did not dare risk another attack against the Americans and the possibility of another Bunker Hill.

On March 17, the British evacuated Boston en mass. Though the celebration among Americans was immense, no one knew better than Washington what a triumph it was. Not only had the Americans beat back the British, but they had beat back the British while in a weak, severely deprived state of affairs: "We have maintained our Ground against the Enemy, under the above want of Powder, and we have disbanded one Army and recruited another, within Musket Shot of two and Twenty Regiments, the Flower of the British Army, when our strength have been little if any, superior to theirs; and, at last, have beat them, in a shameful and precipitate manner out of a place the strongest by Nature on this Continent, and strengthend and fortified in the best manner and at an enormous Expence."

Chapter Twenty-Two:
Colonial Victories Elsewhere

By that time in March, the patriots had taken full control of all thirteen colonies, and even a British outpost in the Bahamas known as New Providence. Esek Hopkins led seven ships in a raid of New Providence to loot its supplies and munitions, but things turned to his favor during the Battle of Nassau on March 3 and 4. So, he decided to expand the raid into an outright attempt to seize the island. He landed two hundred and fifty Marines and sailors. Under the covering fire of the *Providence* and *Wasp* ships of the Continental Fleet, the assault overwhelmed Fort Montague. American forces pursued the retreating British soldiers to Fort Nassau, where the British surrendered. The British managed to evacuate most of the gunpowder that the Americans had been after, but the Continental Fleet still captured an important British outpost, as well as eighty-eight cannons and fifteen mortars.

The next month, Congress decided to consolidate these military gains with some more progress in the political sphere, and instructed the colonies to lay the groundwork for major declarations in the summer of 1776 by drafting up state constitutions that threw off their allegiances to the British Crown.

Getting desperate, King George III began pressing on whatever Native American tribes he could to strike at the Americans from the west. These efforts came to fruition in late June and early July, when Cherokees attacked along the entire southern front. The Cherokee attacks brought up a general Indian offensive that hit South Carolina especially hard. Cherokee Beloved Woman Nancy Ward leaked the Cherokee invasion plans to an American trader by the name of Isaac Thoma. Thus, while American forces were strategically caught by surprise, they at least were tactically ready to stand their ground wherever possible, then drive off the Indian raids back to the east of the Appalachian Mountains.

Section Three:
1776-1777, American Victories Give Way to the British Empire's Might

Chapter Twenty-Three:
The String of American Victories Begin to Falter

King George III now expanded his earlier treason declaration to now include anyone serving in the Continental Army. But his angry words had little effect at this point – on the colonialists in particular, but even on his own generals, who treated captured colonialists as prisoners of war and refused to conduct any trials for treason. Not one American was ever put on trial for treason against the Crown. British generals would come to rely on loyalists in the British Americas, after all, and they knew that harsh treatment of prisoners of war would result in reprisals and expulsions of loyalists in the thirteen colonies. Still, "harsh" is a relative term, as the British maltreatment of American prisoners resulted in more American deaths in prisoner of war camps than on the battlefield.

By the summer of 1776 the Crown's actual representatives were no longer in control of anything south of Canada. The thirteen states had all adopted their own constitutions, thus throwing off any allegiances to the Crown and granting themselves the legal authority to help Congress formally declare independence. The American declaration of independence was at hand. The Second Continental Congress first began meeting on May 10, 1775 – on the same day that Benedict Arnold was sent up to capture Fort Ticonderoga's artillery for the siege of Boston. By the summer of 1776, the Second Continental Congress decided that the time had come to write the Declaration of Independence, the document that would introduce the thirteen colonies into the international community as their own government. Declaring independence would be not only a major morale boost and a major unifier for the otherwise thirteen distinct colonies, but would also give major powers like France and Spain another reason to increase their support of the American war effort.

However, the United States Declaration of Independence was not originally a goal that most delegates had in mind when they first showed up to the Second Continental Congress's May meeting in 1775. Some delegates hoped for eventual independence, but no one said a word about it. Most delegates believed that this conflict was Parliament's fault, and that King George would step in on the Americans' behalf to put an end to Parliament's overreaching and un-British policies. These delegates were sorely disappointed when King George III instead rejected Congress's second petition, issued his Proclamation of Rebellion, and openly announced that he would bring foreign assistance (read: brutal German mercenaries) into the conflict. Some members of Parliament balked, objecting on the grounds that these harsh measures were not only making reconciliation hopeless, but were driving the American rebellion into an all-out revolution for independence.

Chapter Twenty-Four:
The Declaration of Independence

That minority opinion in Parliament was exactly right. Soon after it was painfully apparent that King George III would not step into this conflict as a conciliator, Thomas Paine published his pamphlet, "Common Sense." This pamphlet did not really introduce any new ideas into the debate, especially among the delegates at the Second Continental Congress, but it was immensely influential in stimulating public debate on and public support for breaking away from Great Britain. Most colonials regarded themselves as British Americans, not as Americans, and independence was a topic that even most patriots had not really given thought to until now, when King George III's harsh words proved that diplomacy and reconciliation was as hopeless as ever. Great Britain issued the Prohibitory Act at this time, blockading American ports and, in the eyes of patriots like John Adams, in effect declaring American independence by bringing about "a complete Dismemberment of the British Empire" before the Americans had a chance to do it for themselves.

After the colonies had finished creating their own constitutions, the Second Continental Congress saw itself as legally able to begin drafting the declaration of independence. On June 11, 1776, they appointed a "Committee of Five" to draft this declaration: Thomas Jefferson of Virginia, John Adams of Massachusetts, Benjamin Franklin of Pennsylvania, Robert R. Livingston of New York, and Roger Sherman of Connecticut. Jefferson led this committee, and his life story would make it clear as to why he, out of so many qualified people, was hand-selected for the job.

Born on April 13, 1743 into Shadwell, Virginia, Thomas Jefferson was third of ten children. Like George Washington, he was of English descent. But unlike Washington, Jefferson grew up with an incredible education, at the hands of tutors, reverends, and at the College of William & Mary in Williamsburg, Virginia. He was an excellent student, both in his youth and throughout his life. As he once told John Adams, "I cannot live without books." He had collected so many books in his personal library that his library would, after his death, go on to grow into the Library of Congress, the second largest library in the world today (the largest is the British Library). In 1767, Jefferson was admitted to the Virginia bar.

While practicing law, he also ran for and won election to the Virginia House of Burgesses in 1769. The House sent him as its representative to the Second Continental Congress in 1775, where he quickly gained people's respect and admiration for his depth of knowledge about eloquence. His young protégé James Madison would soon go on to become the architect of the U.S. Constitution, thus earning his place as one of the key figures in the new nation's founding.

After being selected to lead the committee in charge of drafting the Declaration of Independence, Jefferson decided to split it into five sections:

First, an Introduction to the republic concept of natural rights ("When in the Course of human events, it becomes necessary for one people to dissolve the political bands which have connected them with another, and to assume among the powers of the earth, the separate and equal station to which the Laws of Nature and of Nature's God entitle them, a decent respect to the opinions of mankind requires that they should declare the causes which impel them to the separation.");

Second, a Preamble to justify when revolution is necessary ("We hold these truths to be self-evident, that all men are created equal, that they are endowed by their Creator with certain unalienable Rights, that among these are Life, Liberty and the pursuit of Happiness.");

Third, an Indictment against Great Britain for forcing the Americans into splitting away from the Crown ("Such has been the patient sufferance of these Colonies; and such is now the necessity which constrains them to alter their former Systems of Government. The history of the present King of Great Britain is a history of repeated injuries and usurpations, all having in direct object the establishment of an absolute Tyranny over these States. To prove this, let Facts be submitted to a candid world.");

Fourth, a Denunciation that proved that the present conditions justified a revolution ("Nor have We been wanting in attentions to our British brethren. We have warned them from time to time of attempts by their legislature to extend an unwarrantable jurisdiction over us. We have reminded them of the circumstances of our emigration and settlement here. We have appealed to their native justice and magnanimity, and we have conjured them by the ties of our common kindred to disavow these usurpations, which, would inevitably interrupt our connections and correspondence. They too have been deaf to the voice of justice and of consanguinity. We must, therefore, acquiesce in the necessity, which denounces our Separation, and hold them, as we hold the rest of mankind, Enemies in War, in Peace Friends.");

And fifth, a Conclusion ("And for the support of this Declaration, with a firm reliance on the protection of divine Providence, we mutually pledge to each other our Lives, our Fortunes and our sacred Honor."), followed by space for the delegates' signatures. After a few minor revisions to soften the language (for instance, Congress cut out Jefferson's claim that Great Britain had forced slavery on the colonies), Congress adopted it on July 4, 1776, creating a new nation in the world – one that called itself the United States of America. John Hancock was the president of the Continental Congress, so he was given the first opportunity to sign this document. The youngest signer was just twenty-six years old, Edward Rutledge.

Chapter Twenty-Five:
The Declaration of Independence is Revealed

Once it was signed, the declaration was sent across the street to John Dunlap's printing shop. By July 8, 1776, the declaration was distributed to the thirteen colonies and was started to be read out loud at the colonies' public squares. Reverend Ezra Stiles wrote passionately: "Thus the Congress has tied a Gordian knot, which the Parliament] will find they can neither cut, nor untie. The thirteen united colonies now rise into an Independent Republic among the kingdoms, states, and empires on earth.... And have I lived to see such an important and astonishing revolution?"

Washington had the declaration loudly read to his troops in New York City, while thousands of British troops watched on helplessly from the harbor. Across the colonies, Americans swept up in a rush of patriotic fervor went around their towns, in search of royalist statutes to tear down and burn. An equestrian statue of King George in New York City was melted into lead that the Continental Army would use for musket balls. Within weeks, the declaration would reach the South American states and the shores of Great Britain, Spain, France, and Germany, then slowly continue eastwards, hitting the public masses with as much inspiration as it hit their overlords with fear.

Today, historians are split over the question of how to interpret the Declaration of Independence. Some argue that the declaration is a philosophical tract about natural rights. Others treat it as a legal document, as basically just an indictment against King George III for violating the British Americans' rights. Still others take a middle ground, regarding the document as both a philosophical tract that applies to all nations and peoples, and also as a legal document specifically against Great Britain – in other words, as the world's first document of international law. Whatever view one takes, it remains a fact that this document has no legally binding effect on the domestic laws of the present-day United States; that is the Constitution's job.

Chapter Twenty-Six:
The Setbacks Begin and a New British Strategy Emerges

Needless to say, Parliament and King George had no interest in recognizing either this declaration or the congress that had adopted it. British hopes for an unstoppable Indian onslaught were dashed as Indian raids throughout July and August were steadily beat back. In South Carolina, at Lyndley's Fort on July 15 and at Seneca on August 1, patriots managed to fend off major ambushes attacks from Indians and loyalists dressed as Indians. More Cherokee attempts at a major victory was soundly defeated by the patriot forces led by Andrew Pickens on August 10 at Tugaloo River, South Carolina, then again on August 12 at the Indian town of Tamassy, which Pickens' forces burned down.

(While it is easy to believe nowadays the Indian were nomadic warriors, the reality is that some Indian tribes had settled down into cities like Cahokia, a Native American city located in present day St. Louis that, in 1250, was larger than London and featured a sophisticated urban center, with satellite villages and thatched-roof houses that lined its central plazas, and with complex trade routes that stretched from the Great Lakes to the Gulf of Mexico).

The British decided upon a new strategy, one that would begin with a British counter-attack through New York City, then continue with a steady march down south of overwhelming British firepower. After the retreat from Boston, most British forces retreated north to their main North American naval base, in Halifax, Nova Scotia. (Some British forces had gone south, hoping to establish a better stronghold in South Carolina, but they were decisively defeated at Fort Moultrie on June 28). King George III began amassing a new contingent of British forces at Halifax.

This base was well out of Washington's reach, and few patriots wanted to repeat the disastrous Canada campaign by attempting to capture this naval base. After amassing, the British forces sailed to New York City in August of 1776. They all arrived on Staten Island with over one hundred ships from the most formidable fleet on the planet.

Chapter Twenty-Seven:
New York City is Ablaze

The fighting over New York City would stretch from August to November, with clashes stretching around Brooklyn, up and down Manhattan's streets and alleys, and up into Harlem. Washington would lose more than three out of four soldiers, and nearly be captured in the end. But the hard-fought lessons that Washington, his officers, and soldiers learned on the streets of New York City helped forged the Continental Army into the professional fighting force it would soon become, through its surprise attacks at Trenton and Princeton against the feared German mercenary forces.

Washington had already marched the larger part of his Boston army out of Boston and into New York, having expected precisely this avenue of attack. At twenty thousand souls, New York's population at this time was certainly larger than Boston's, but smaller than the City of Philadelphia's. One of Washington's top commanders reported, upon his initial inspection of the city, that the city's culture was nothing like Boston's. Instead, he found that, "The people—why the people are magnificent: in their carriages, which are numerous, in their house furniture, which is fine, in their pride and conceit, which are inimitable, in their profaneness, which is intolerable, in the want of principle, which is prevalent, in their Toryism, which is insufferable."

On August 22, the redcoats began their march into Long Island. By August 27, the redcoats trapped George Washington's forces in Long Island. Washington had not slept in two days and had been constantly on horseback, but he rallied his trapped and panicking soldiers together, telling them, "The Enemy have now landed on Long Island, and the hour is fast approaching, on which the Honor and Success of this army, and the safety of our bleeding Country depend. Remember officers and Soldiers, that you are Freemen, fighting for the blessings of Liberty--that slavery will be your portion, and that of your posterity, if you do not acquit yourselves like men: Remember how your Courage and Spirit have been despised, and traduced by your cruel invaders; though they have found by dear experience at Boston, Charlestown and other places, what a few brave men contending in their own land, and in the best of causes can do, against base hirelings and mercenaries – Be cool, but determined; do not fire at a distance, but wait for orders from your officers."

Chapter Twenty-Eight:
Comparing the Armies

The Continental Army and the redcoats could not have been more different. Where the British regulars in red were in their late twenties, the Americans in homespun clothes were in their early twenties. Where both the Americans and redcoats had been farmers, unskilled laborers, and other tradesmiths before finding themselves recruited into their respective armies, the Americans had little to no military experience prior to the siege of Boston, except for those who belonged to a typically casual militia made up of cousins and distant relatives.

Where both the Americans and British were intensely proud of their heritage of their army, New Englanders were notoriously reluctant to wash their own clothes, but, as one newspaper observed, "Among the regular troops [redcoats] every private soldier is obliged to put on a clean shirt twice, perhaps three times a week, according to the season and climate; and there are a certain number of officers appointed every day to see that each man washes his own linen, if he had not a woman to do it for him."

As would become his habit through this war, Washington managed to retreat his army successfully out of Long Island under the cover of the night. In an unexpected turn of events, Washington's army fell into shambles as soon as it landed on New York Island, as masses of American troops took off to go home, visit friends, and for numerous other reasons leave their post. Many of them had been recruited, since part of the Boston force had to be left there. And Washington observed that the laidback newcomers' attitude was contagious, as the newcomers' arrival was loosening the discipline in the regulars: the militia "have infected another part of the Army. Their want of discipline and refusal of almost every kind of restraint & Government, have produce a like Conduct" in the regulars from Boston. Even at this point in the war, Washington was clearly still getting used to being the commander of a rather unorthodox military force.

Chapter Twenty-Nine:
The Fight for New York City Stalls

The British came into the rest of New York City on September 15, but their entrance came as no surprise to Washington's forces. That is because Washington had called for a spy to go behind British lines and discover where they intended to land in New York City, and one man stepped forward: Nathan Hale. The militiamen lieutenant from Connecticut went behind enemy lines and reported on their movements for much of September, a crucial advantage in Washington's preparations. Hale was discovered in mid-September, however, and sent to 66th Street and Third Avenue to be hung.

Both American and British accounts described the man, only twenty-one years of age at the time, as conducting himself honorably and eloquently. When asked for his last words, he will forever be remembered in American lore as having said, "I only regret that I have but one life to lose for my country." Others say he said, "I am so satisfied with the cause in which I have engaged that my only regret is that I have not more lives than one to offer in its service." Still others remember hearing him recite the passage from Joseph Addison's play, *Cato*, which many

Whigs found inspirational: "How beautiful is death, when earned by virtue! Who would not be that youth? What pity is it, that we can die but once to serve our country."

After the British landed in New York, they then struck out at the American forces at Harlem Heights on September 16. In an unexpected turn of events, American forces under Washington, Nathanael Greene, and Israel Putnam hold their ground at the Battle of Harlem Heights. One soldier described the action excitedly in his journal: "I saw one man tumble from his horse—never did I take better aim at a bird—yet I know not that I killed any or touched any. The fire was returned and they killed two of our men dead, none wounded. It became proper for us to retreat and we retreated about four hundred yards and were joined by Captain Atlee's regiment."

On the other end of the gunfire, a British soldier described the ferocious exchange of volleys as well, his words echoing the turmoil and chaos of the surprising reversal of fortunes from the British perspective: "I called to my men to run to the first wall they could find and we all set off, some into some short bushes, others straight across a field...[and] in running across the field we [were] exposed to the fire of 300 men. We had literally run out in the midst [of them] and they calling to me to surrender. I stopped twice to look behind me and saw the riflemen so thick and not one of my own men. I made for the wall as hard as I could drive and they peppering at me...at last I gained the wall and threw myself headlong."

The American victory at Harlem Heights was an unexpected turn of events in most people's eyes, but not everyone was so surprised. Washington and his top generals had selected New York not in the hopes of actually defending it in the long-run, because they had decided early on that they could not defend it without control of the sea. Instead, their goal in holding New York was to deliver another, bigger Bunker Hill kind of victory to the British – a victory, in the end, but a very costly one.

Chapter Thirty:
The Fight for New York City Takes a Turn for the Worse

Over time, as Washington and others had predicted, the Colonial Army's ten thousand soldiers could not withstand the thirty-two thousand British regulars all around them (forty thousand British regulars, if one includes the sailors and warships among their number), as well as, for the first time, a large number of German mercenaries fighting under the British. With armies of this size, it was easily the largest battle that had ever taken place in the history of North America.

Indeed, there were more redcoats in New York City than there were New Yorkers. There were even more redcoats than there were citizens in America's largest city, Philadelphia, which housed around thirty thousand Americans. One New Yorker, Joseph Reed, wrote down what he saw with powerful, vivid imagery:

When I look down, and see the prodigious fleet they have collected, I cannot help but be astonished that a people should come 3000 miles at such risk trouble and expense to rob, plunder and destroy another people because they will not lay their lives and fortune at their feet.

The redcoats and their mercenaries put their numerical superiority to their advantage, descending over the Americans, using their overwhelming numbers to attack from the front and from the left side. This forced Washington back, and again trapped his forces in New York City. Out of good options, Washington called for a daring, risky nightmare retreat, considered one of the greatest military accomplishments of his career. British officers "in the morning, to our great astonishment, found they had evacuated all their works on Brookland...with not a shot being fired at them...neither could our shipping get up for want of wind, and the whole escaped..." Other officers said that they were surprised but not surprised as well, considering what a shock it had been a few months ago to wake up on morning in Boston as see the cannons from Fort Ticonderoga, of all places, on the hills overlooking Boston.

Had the British prevented his retreat, as they had expected, then Washington's army would eventually have had to surrender. Such a momentous loss to the American cause would likely have ended the Revolution itself, and this stinging defeat, as one American officer observed was not at all an unlikely scenario: "To move so large a body of troops, with all their necessary appendages, across a river a full mile wide, with a rapid current, in the face of a victorious well disciplined army nearly three times as numerous as his own, and a fleet capable of stopping the navigation so that not one boat could have passed over, seemed to present most formidable obstacles."

Chapter Thirty-One:
The Long American Retreat Begins

The retreat began as a retreat from New York City, but ultimately expanded throughout November as a retreat from New York entirely, through New Jersey and even Pennsylvania. This came hand in hand with a string of American reversals elsewhere. Cherokee attacks in North Carolina gained ground against Colonel Williamson's patriots, and Benedict Arnold saw a stinging defeat at the Battle of Valcour Island, around Lake Champlain.

Many patriots had been religiously motivated, and felt that God would aid in the American Revolution to make up for anything the revolutionaries lacked. This turn for the worse suggested that divine providence might not be on their side, as one commentator in the *New England Chronicle* lamented: "We have thought God was for us, and had given many and signal instances of his power and mercy in our favor, and had greatly frowned upon and disappointed our enemies; and verily it has been so. But have we repented and given him the glory? Verily no. His hand seems to be turned and stretched out against us—and strong is his hand."

Aggravated that Washington had slipped their grasp, the British called for a peace negotiation. Congress sent a delegation that included John Adams and Benjamin Franklin to Staten Island. The Staten Island Peace Conference lasted only a few hours, with the British General Howe doing most of the talking. The American delegation listened patiently, knowing that even if the conference came to nothing, at least the pause in hostilities meant some badly-needed breathing space for the Continental Army. General Howe turned to insisting on the retraction of the Declaration of Independence, and the conference quickly broke down. Cross-Atlantic relations had strained well beyond the point of reconciliation, and the Declaration of Independence, as the Crown now learned the hard way, was here to stay.

Chapter Thirty-Two:
The Retreat Ends and Washington Establishes His Spy Network

In Pennsylvania, the Continental Army stood its ground, unwilling to cede yet another colony to the imperial forces. As 1776 wore on into winter, the passing months saw the northern portion of New England falling at an alarmingly rapid pace. In the middle of drafting the Articles of Confederation, the Second Continental Congress had to even move from Philadelphia to Baltimore, lest British soldiers storm into the meeting one day and capture virtually all of the American Revolution's leaders in one swoop. Meanwhile, British forces turned New York City into their headquarters, and would hold onto it firmly until they were forced to surrender it at the end of the war in 1783.

Making the best of a desperate situation, Washington took full advantage of New York City's centrality to the British war effort by turning it into the focal point of his intelligence network. As a general, Washington placed immense important on spies, intelligence reports, and secret knowledge of the enemy. The very first account entered into his account book, in fact, was for three hundred thirty-three dollars and thirty-three cents for a spy "to go into Boston [during the Boston Siege] for the purpose of conveying intelligence of the enemy's movements and designs."

With such focus on intelligence and knowledge, one would not have predicted that Washington had been born in the small town of Tidewater, Virginia on February 11, 1732, and grew up with very little formal education. Washington grew up as an outdoorsy boy, an explorer of backcountry western Virginia. In fact, his lack of interest in books and studying led to his passion for exploring and taming the great outdoors of Virginia. When he was only eleven years old, Washington's father died, leaving him as a fatherless little boy with no wealth and little prospects in a Virginian society in which everyone was a plantation laborer, a plantation owner, or a merchant. The politicians were all wealthy plantation owners, so that profession was certainly not an open option to Washington. Clearly, Washington grew up in an environment that taught him on a daily basis that little would come easily for him; if he wanted to leave a mark on this world, he would have to struggle to earn that recognition.

Washington was up for the challenge. Taking full advantage of his incredible height and his love of the outdoors, he turned to the Virginia militia instead of becoming just another plantation laborer or merchant. The pay was meager, but Washington served for the sake of service. As he wrote to a friend, Colonel Fairfax, the complaints from his fellow officers about the lack of reasonable pay for service were "founded on strict Reason, [but] for my own part, it is a matter almost indifferent whether I serve for full pay or as a generous volunteer; indeed, did my circumstances correspond with my inclinations, I should not hesitate a moment to prefer the latter; for the motives that have led me here are pure and noble. I had no view of acquisition but that of honor, by serving faithfully my king and country."

With this selfless attitude, as well as his formidable physique and courage in the face of adversity, it would come as little surprise that Washington quickly rose through the ranks. He became a major by the young age of twenty, an unusual feat even at that time. As a major, he had his first command position and was entrusted with his first combat mission – namely, fighting the French military forces around the Allegheny River valley. It proved to be a disappointment. As capable as he was on his own, leadership was a challenge because he could not go out and meet the enemy on his own anymore; he had to guide others towards the goal. In his first combat engagement, his control of his forces slipped out of his hands, and the battle ended up being a chaotic, individualistic fight instead of a cohesive fight with any clear direction.

Washington had taught himself how to write, and, undaunted by this setback, he wrote a book, *The Journal of Major George Washington. The Journal* recounted his daring adventures during this time, and, as an author, he certainly had a way of writing the captured people's attention. "I heard the bullets whistle; and believe me there is something charming in the sound," he wrote, with all the bravado of a thrill-seeking kid, seeming in the eyes of the colonists to be their poster boy. The book spread his feats throughout the Thirteen Colonies, and helped him receive his next major task.

Washington and his forces encountered French troops and their Indian allies at Great Meadows, Virginia, where Washington's poor judgment and inexperience led to a bloody, backwoods, embarrassing defeat – humble beginnings for the man who would go on to become the commander in chief of the entire Continental Army, then the first president of the world's first and only republic, the only nation to be born during the Enlightenment.

Chapter Thirty-Three:
Logistics Start to Cripple the American War Effort

Another major issue in the war, as in any major war, was the question of finances. Great Britain could afford to pay for the war that would end up costing it about ten billion dollars in today's money, because Great Britain had long-ago established one of the world's most sophisticated financial systems. Based on the wealth of Great Britain's landowners, the Empire had little trouble raising the necessary taxes to pay the logistics suppliers, tens of thousands of foreign mercenaries, and tens of thousands of British soldiers and sailors. The British tax system collected close to twelve percent of the Gross Domestic Product in taxes during the American Revolution, in addition to borrowing about forty percent of the money it needed.

King George III had also inherited a blatantly mercenary economic system in which bribery, favoritism, and corruption was blatantly rampant – not only in politics, but in British society in general. King George III had not created this system, but he knew how to use it to great effect when he needed extra funds at short notice and the regular channels could not supply these funds. Clergyman Tobias Smollet described London as "the devil's drawing room," and Jonathan Swift made Great Britain's corruption a favorite subject in numerous writings.

France also had an efficient tax system, but could not hide the fact that its tax system was not as well-developed as Britain's when heavy spending brought the French close to bankruptcy and revolution. Given the immense costs that the British paid and the near-collapse of the French monarchy, it would come as little surprise that the new American Congress struggled immensely in funding the war. Congress certainly did not have ten billion dollars lying around on the floor, though it helped that the American costs of the war would amount to "only" about one hundred million dollars. At most, the colonies had twelve million dollars in gold. The British blockade of goods coming into America ports worsened the situation considerably by cutting off virtually all imports from and exports to the outside world.

Congress began by relying on volunteer support from militiamen and from donations. Many of the Nation's founders – especially Samuel Adams, Patrick Henry, John Adams, Benjamin Franklin, Thomas Jefferson, Thomas Paine, George Washington, James Madison and Alexander Hamilton – were strong believers in republican values that citizens were required to put their civic duties ahead of their personal desires. Still, volunteerism from the public would not be nearly enough. Congress went on to delay actual payments, pay soldiers (who typically made eight dollars a month in 18th century currency) in depreciated currency when it got around to paying soldiers, and make endless promises about post-war payments.

The appointment of Robert Morris as Superintendent of Finance of the United States in 1781 proved to be a turning point in American financial struggles. Morris hit the ground running by seriously cutting wasteful and unnecessary spending, and quickly creating the efficient tax system that the fledgling new United States needed.

Chapter Thirty-Four:
Washington's Launches into the Offensive

Late that December, Washington decided to meet the continued onslaught into New Jersey and Pennsylvania with a fateful surprise attack of his own. He'd received an unsolicited letter from a lowly sergeant in the Pennsylvania militia, Joseph Reed, who gave him an ingenious idea for giving the Americans a sudden victory as a Christmas present:

Will it not be possible, my dear General, for our troops or such part of them as can act with advantage to make a diversion or something more at or about Trenton? The greater the alarm, the more likely success will attend the attacks....

I will not disguise my own sentiments that our cause is desperate and hopeless if we do not take the opp[ortunit]y of the collection of troops at present to strike some stroke. Our affairs are hastening fast to ruin if we do not retrieve them by some happy event. Delay with us is now equal to total defeat.

It was a bold idea, certainly. The Americans had for weeks been retreating; they were in tattered shape, worn out, and ill fed. How could such a force be sent onto the offensive? Washington called his senior generals to meet him on Christmas Eve, and they decided upon the plan to attack. This decision took his own staff by as much surprise as it would surprise their enemies, because Washington was a great thinker, a great speaker, and a great administrator – but the ferocity of a warrior is the kind of attitude it takes to order a surprise attack, and the perennially cool-headed Washington was not known for such ferocity. Offensive actions, unlike the defensive actions around Boston and New York, also required an extreme tolerance for ambiguity and risk, which is precisely the opposite of what a good administrator can tolerate.

Nonetheless, the die was cast. Washington had tasted from the bitter fruit of defeat before – indeed, his first battle was a defeat, and the majority of his skirmishes against Indians during the 1750s were defeats – but he had learned that even when he was defeated as a commander, he did not have to be defeated as a man. With that in mind, Washington then famously crossed the Delaware River into New Jersey and, in the dead of night, defeated Great Britain's mercenary force of Hessians at Trenton on December 26 and, on January 3, at Princeton as well.

The German mercenaries were as feared as they were hated, because their fighting style was particularly vicious. Even the British looked at the Hessians in particular with some distain, with one British officer writing in a letter, "The Hessians and our Highlanders gave no quarters [the letter read], and it was a fine thing to see with what alacrity they dispatched the rebels with their bayonets after we had surrendered them so that they could not resist.... You know all stratagems are lawful in war, especially against such vile enemies to their King and country."

Chapter Thirty-Five:
Commander Rall's Fateful Decision at Trenton

In one of the stories that history books often forget to mention, the addiction among British officers to card games played a large role in the reversal of fortunes at Trenton and Princeton. Johann Gottlieb Rall commanded the Hessian barracks at Trenton, and according to some accounts he was apparently in the middle of a very interesting cardgame at the Christmas party when a loyalist came over to hand him a note. As the note said, the loyalist had seen Washington gathering his forces in a surprise attack. Rall took the note, thanked the loyalist, then proceeded to place the note directly into his pocket without even giving it a look. The loyalist warned him to look at it, because the Americans were coming. But Rall sent him off anyway, telling him he would read the note soon.

Rall failed to do so. It was too inconceivable to him that the disorganized, badly beaten colonials would even be able to mount an attack. As Rall had said the day before, "Those clodhoppers will not attack us!" At Boston and New York and throughout their retreat, they had been consistently on the retreat. Were they even capable of an attack? Meanwhile, Washington entered the boat to cross the Delaware, nudging his three-hundred-pound Colonel Henry Knox with the immortal order: "Shift that fat ass, Harry. But slowly, or you'll swamp the damn boat."

At daybreak, Washington and his troops attacked. The freezing sleet and freezing cold early morning temperature had made it difficult to spot the Americans approaching the camp, and the Hessians retreated in a full route; resistance was hopeless. Nearly one thousand Hessian mercenaries were captured. Rall himself was struck in the body by a musket ball when he was leading the retreat from Trenton.

A surgeon cut open his clothes to treat his wounds, and out into the snow fell the note that warned of Washington's approach. Had Rall taken the time to read this note, the war may have turned out very differently, with him living to see it end, and perhaps even being the one to capture Washington in the end. Rall lived just long enough to read the note, and his reported last words were poignant, mournful ones: "If I had read this, I would not be here."

As one might imagine, the British and colonial reaction was once again one of total shock and disbelief:

I did not wait to hear anything more said, but dropped the basket and ran out into the street and passed two [British] sentinels that I had given the countersign on my way to the store. Though they challenged me, I did not stop, but ran as fast as I could to my quarters.... By the time I got home I was quite out of breath and ran into the room where the officers were sitting around the table. Several of them asked what's the matter, and as soon as I could recover breath to speak I spoke with considerable emphasis: "General Washington has defeated the Hessians at Trenton this morning and has taken 900 prisoners and six pieces of artillery."

"Who told you so?"

I could not tell as I did not know the gentleman's name, but I told them it was where I purchased the groceries.... At which some of the officers laughed and asked me various questions, while others did not say a word and looked very serious, as if doubting the news, and others thought it too good to be true.

Chapter Thirty-Six:
The Aftermath of Trenton and Princeton

These successful surprise attacks allowed the Continental Army to recapture most of New Jersey, and, more importantly, gave a badly-needed morale boost to the patriots when their prospects of victory seemed as bleak as ever. Reenlistments during this crucial period, when the enlistment period was coming to an end, finally starting going up. One farmer captured the colonial mood swing in his journal, writing, "Six weeks ago [we were] lamenting the unhappy situation of the Americans and pitying the wretched condition of their much-beloved General, supposing his want of skill and experience in military matters had brought them all to the brink of destruction. In short all was gone, all was lost. But not the scale is turned and Washington's name is extolled to the clouds."

Washington's journal and the writings of the men around him also indicates that the general himself had gotten a badly needed morale boost of his own; he began to lead with more confidence from this day onwards, and came to the conclusion that he was equal to the demands of his formidable assignment.

The victories at Trenton and Princeton were, in other words, not only strategically useful in recapturing New Jersey, but also symbolically crucial in transforming the meaning of the American Revolution into a cause that could be won.

Section Four: 1777-1781, Stalemate in the North and the Empire's Southern Campaign

Chapter Thirty-Seven: 1777 and a New British Strategy

British forces began the year 1777 with a new grand strategy. The beginning of 1777 marked the second year of a war that the British had predicted would last just a few months, and the British were eager to fulfill what Secretary for the American Colonies Lord George Germain had promised: to end the rebellion with a decisive blow, the kind of decisive blow that had so embarrassingly slipped through their hands at the Battle of Brooklyn. British forces believed that New England was the primary source of the patriots' support, in large part because so much of the pre-war agitation – just to name a few: the Boston Massacre, the Sons of Liberty, and the Boston Tea Party – had taken place in Boston, Massachusetts.

The British therefore decided that their next major offensive would have the aim of sealing off New England from the Continental

Army, because New England appeared to be the heart of the patriots' support. A major British invasion force swooped in through Canada while the British army stationed in New York drove into Philadelphia and seized it from the Continental Army. It was all part of a grand plan to split the colonies up through a three-way pincer movement: the western pincer would go through Ontario into western New York with ten thousand soldiers, Indians, loyalists, and camp followers; the southern pincer would go up the Hudson River from New York City; and the north pincer would head south from Montreal.

These three pincers would meet around Albany, New York, thus cutting New England from the colonies below. The only downside of the plan is that Washington, who was somewhere in northern New Jersey, might take this as an opportunity to retake New York City, so General Howe sent an additional force to Philadelphia, where it would keep Washington distracted with Philadelphia's defense.

That plan failed. It failed so miserably that the Americans would receive a major victory at the Battle of Saratoga, another turning point in the American Revolution. On September 19, 1777, British General John Burgoyne struck a small but costly victory over American forces led by General Horatio Gates. Burgoyne trailed them as they retreated to Bemis Heights, at which point George Washington nervously sent along his best infantry commander to aid in the heights' defenses – Benedict Arnold. Burgoyne then made the fatal mistake of attacking them again at the heights on October 7.

Chapter Thirty-Eight:
The Battle of Saratoga and the End of Fighting in the North

Burgoyne was the commander who had recaptured Fort Ticonderoga from the Americans with laughable ease. Having just kicked the American force back again, perhaps his overconfidence was understandable. This time, however his overconfidence proved to be too much. His attack against the heights proved to be too costly even to his superior numbers. At one crucial moment in the battle, Arnold Benedict found himself watching on the sidelines as the Americans and British forces fought it out for control of the ground. Just hours earlier, Arnold had been sidelined for quarrelling with General Horatio Gates, the overall commander of these colonial forces. Seeing the battle at its turning point, Arnold couldn't stay away.

Arnold reportedly downed a slug of rum, the leaped onto a nearby horse and raced into the front lines. Colonials rallied around him as he galloped from one part of the field to another, leading devastating charges into a teetering British line. At one point, he was waiving his sword around so wildly that he sliced one of his own officers. A bullet shattered his leg and brought him off his horse, just as the redcoats began retreating.

The American forces were now the ones trailing him to his defenses, and surrounded him. After ten days of being encircled, Burgoyne had little choice but to surrender. In their acceptance of this surrender, the American forces came in playing an awfully familiar tune, the Yankee Doodle. As British officer Tom Anbury recalled at Saratoga, "It was not a little mortifying to hear them play this tune, when their army marched down to our surrender."

Overjoyed at the news of not just a major American triumph, but *the* greatest American triumph in the war effort so far, Congress issued a proclamation for a national day "for solemn Thanksgiving and praise," the first American holiday observance with the name "Thanksgiving." At this point in the war, one might notice that Washington's speeches changed in tone. Where he and other officers had often appealed to pride, heroism, and honor in their earlier speeches, his speeches now broadened subtly to include even larger topics:

This army—the main American Army— will certainly not suffer itself to be out done by their northern Brethren—they will never endure such disgrace; but with an ambition becoming freemen, contending in the most righteous cause, rival the heroic spirit which swelled their bosoms, and which so nobly exerted, has procured them deathless renown. Covet! my Countrymen, and fellow soldiers! Covet! a share of the glory due to heroic deeds!

Let it never be said, that in a day of action, you turned your backs on the foe—let the enemy no longer triumph—They brand you with ignominious epithets—Will you patiently endure that reproach? Will you suffer the wounds given to your Country to go unrevenged? Will you resign your parents—wives—children and friends to be the wretched vassals of a proud, insulting foe? And your own necks to the halter?

Chapter Thirty-Nine:
Bacterial Disaster at Valley Forge

British soldiers in Pennsylvania had their hands tied at a siege at Fort Mifflin, allowing Washington to consolidate his victory at Saratoga without having to fend off any major counter-attacks, and preserve his Continental Army at their New Jersey winter quarters at Valley Forge, Pennsylvania. Washington picked this valley instead of the numerous other suitable locations because it was close enough to the British to stop them from raiding and foraging deep into Pennsylvania, but still far enough away to prevent the British from being able to mount any surprise attacks.

If the British wanted to launch an attack anyway, despite their lack of surprise, then the densely forested plateau of Mount Joy and Mount Misery, along with the Schuylkill River to the north, would give the British offensive a nightmare of natural obstacles to overcome. The forest was also useful for making the thousands of log huts that Washington's army needed.

Unfortunately, the Colonial Army did not only have the British to fight off. Over two thousand five hundred soldiers died that winter.

Washington's army, for all its offensive feats and incredible ability to evade capture even when trapped and surrounded, was poorly equipped and weary. Only one out of three soldiers actually had shoes, and the long string of bloody footprints that they left behind in their march to Valley Forge spoke volumes of the desperate supply situation beleaguering the Colonial Army at the time.

Even for those who had shoes, the marching often wore those shoes out, and those shoes were seldom replaced – they were just destroyed, and the soldier would have go to on without shoes. Clothes were also subject to normal wear and tear. But unlike shoes, soldiers could go onto the battlefield naked of their clothes. Upwards of four thousand Continental soldiers had to be discharged as unfit for duty when their clothes simply became too tattered to wear, and were unable to be replaced.

Soldiers arrived with little or no rations. Once at the camp, they did not receive much by way of meat and bread either, with many only getting their nourishment from "firecake," a tasteless mix of flour and water. There were not nearly enough blankets to go around during the harsh winter. Aware of the logistics crisis but unable to do anything to make things better,

Washington despaired "that unless some great and capital change suddenly takes place...this Army must inevitably...starve, dissolve, or disperse, in order to obtain subsistence in the best manner they can."

The animals had it even worse, and some seven hundred horses under the Continental Army's control had perished by the end of winter. Though Washington struggled with logistics questions since he first stepped into his appointment as commander in chief on July 3, 1775, the threat of systemic collapse was worse now than ever before.

Chapter Forty:
A Very Deadly Winter Sets In

Given the poor conditions that closed quarters military encampments in general created at that time, and the contributions of malnourishment and general military inexperience, it should come as little surprise that disease and sickness ravaged the population at Valley Forge. Some of the main killers that thrived in the valley that winter were typhoid, typhus, smallpox, dysentery, and pneumonia. Making matters worse, these diseases were not well understood at the time. Doctors and nurses gave the vague diagnosis of "camp fever" to cover what was actually a wide array of distinct, highly infectious, deadly scourges.

Dysentery had afflicted military camps since the dawn of war, such that even the ancient Greek historian Herodotus wrote of dysentery. Typhus, meanwhile, brought high fevers, severe headaches, and delirium to those afflicted with it. Typhus came from lice and fleas, which were in abundance with most armies of that time period. *Salmonella typhosa* often snuck into camp food or water because food and water was kept too closely to sewage water, and this brought about typhoid fever in countless thousands of people, characterized by raging fevers, vomiting, large rashes, excruciating abdominal pain, and diarrhea. Thomas Paine, pained by the sight of so much suffering yet also inspired by the undaunted resolution among the Americans who fought on, had this in mind when he wrote the memorable lines:

THESE are the times that try men's souls. The summer soldier and the sunshine patriot will, in this crisis, shrink from the service of their country; but he that stands by it now, deserves the love and thanks of man and woman. Tyranny, like hell, is not easily conquered; yet we have this consolation with us, that the harder the conflict, the more glorious the triumph. What we obtain too cheap, we esteem too lightly: it is dearness only that gives every thing its value.

Heaven knows how to put a proper price upon its goods; and it would be strange indeed if so celestial an article as FREEDOM should not be highly rated. Britain, with an army to enforce her tyranny, has declared that she has a right (not only to TAX) but "to BIND us in ALL CASES WHATSOEVER" and if being bound in that manner, is not slavery, then is there not such a thing as slavery upon earth. Even the expression is impious; for so unlimited a power can belong only to God.

The camp diseases were so infectious that parents, children, siblings, nurses, and other visitors to Valley Forge would catch one disease or another, then bring it back to their town and lay waste to numerous New England towns. One church in Danbury, Connecticut – despite its apparent separation from the battles of the war effort – lost one hundred parishioners to camp fever by mere November. It certainly did not help matters, for civilians and soldiers alike, that the prevailing cultural norms in New England at the time regarded the washing of clothes as women's work, so men largely avoided washing their own clothes.

When women left the towns to tend to soldiers, the men's dirty cloths would often catch and spread the disease. When women left the military camps to go back home, the New Englander soldiers at the camps would leave their clothes unwashed and succumb to whatever diseases were caught into their garments. As one New Englander observed, after observing the American camp from afar: "They would rather let their clothes rot upon their backs than be at the trouble of cleaning 'em themselves."

Disease, malnourishment, and exposure to freezing temperatures killed the lion's share of the two thousand and five hundred soldiers who perished. Governor Morris of New York described the Continentals as a "skeleton of an army...in a naked, starving condition, out of health, out of spirits." The losses were so grave and so damaging to morale that Washington decided not to go on any offensives for the next few months, even until May.

Instead, Washington focused on their main enemy: disease. He declared a long list of cleanliness rules, and made sure that the new regulations were carefully enforced by going on horseback and reviewing the soldiers every day. He made an example out of rule breakers, subjecting them to severe punishment (flogging, typically) or public humiliation. He also promised them ten dollars' pay per month for whoever reenlisted, despite having no authority to make such a promise.

Chapter Forty-One:
The Confidence in George Washington is Shaken

Washington also repeatedly petitioned for supplies, but the Continental Congress had none to provide. The suffering and lack of supplies was thinning ranks not only by getting many soldiers sick and leaving other soldiers dead, but also by persuading soldiers to not reenlist. Out of eleven regiments, which was about ten thousand men, only one thousand had agreed to stay in November. Washington implored Congress to help with the desperate matter of reenlistments, a subject that the congress members had heard him far more often than they desired. Congress responded with an authorization to raise sixteen more regiments, but that authorization did not exactly bring more people into camp.

Washington therefore had to come up with an ingenious idea, something besides the patriotic speeches that all of the officers were delivering to boost reenlistment rates. Washington decided to create the sixteen new regiments by handpicking their most senior officers. Even the lowliest lieutenant had a shot at suddenly becoming a colonel, if Washington wanted it that way. To have a shot at having the honors of being named a senior officer, however, the officers first had to reenlist.

Once Washington selected his new senior officers, he then allowed them to select the officers they wanted as subordinates, thus perpetuating the cycle of appointments and reenlistments. Being "appointed" a soldier was far less of an honor, so Washington convinced the congress members to promise one hundred acres – which would presumably be cut out of the unsettled western frontiers – to any volunteers and re-enlisters.

These techniques helped boost the number of reenlisted soldiers and officers up to 2,540 by the end of November, but that number was still low enough to be "truly alarming," in Washington's own words. It certainly did not help matters when Washington insisted that not every volunteer could be accepted into the Continental Army. Nobody under seventeen years of age and nobody over fifty years of age would be accepted, and nobody with physical infirmities would be accepted under any circumstances.

Nobody of "insufficient stature" (nobody who was too short in other words) could be accepted, and no deserters from the British army could be accepted. No Tories could be accepted, and nobody who was "lukewarm" to the American cause could be accepted. His newly-minted colonels were eager to fill the ranks of their units, but these regulations made it quite hard to do so, and forced them to turn away hundreds if not thousands of volunteers.

At the end of December, a winter storm fell across New England, bringing the temperatures to the low twenties. Meanwhile, thousands of new British regulars arrived to Boston, bringing along with them King George III's October fiery speech that declared the rioting a rebellion. Helpfully, though, the hatred of England that this speech inspired among the soldiers helped boost reenlistment numbers far more than any patriotic inspiration from Washington.

Soldiers, officers, congressmen, and many members of the public began to question Washington's ability to lead, for the first time. Washington took this criticism to heart, as he had largely been seen as one of the most unifying figures in the American Revolution. Indeed, he would go on to become president by a unanimous vote of confidence, which would become the first and likely the last time that a

United States president would win by such impressive margins.

The mounting criticism of Washington voices people's impatience with the lack of progress on the war effort, and the recent string of losses. People wondered if perhaps Washington had grown too old or tired or out of touch to lead, and if perhaps General Horatio Gates (victor of the Battle of Saratoga) should become commander in chief.

Washington himself had his doubts. In one of his most forlorn letters, he wrote at time of suffering many sleepless nights, saying, "The reflection upon my situation and that of this army produces many an uneasy hour when all around me are wrapped in sleep. Few people know the predicament we are in." With the winter adding to the Americans' long string of defeats, nothing seemed to give the American soldiers or their leaders any reason for hope.

Concerned, Washington replied with uncharacteristic fury that "I can assure those Gentlemen that it is a much easier and less distressing thing to draw remonstrances in a comfortable room by a good fire side than to occupy a cold bleak hill and sleep under frost and Snow without Cloaths or Blankets; however, although they seem to have little feeling for the naked, and distressed Soldier, I feel superabundantly for them, and from my Soul pity those miseries, [which], it is neither in my power to relieve or prevent."

Despite the impossibility of mounting any offensive during the winter and during the rampant diseases that ravished Valley Forge, and despite the fact that Congress had sown the roots of this problem by creating an army in 1775 without actually having investigated what a professional standing army should look like or require, a group led by Brigadier General Thomas Conway attempted to oust Washington in exchange for General Horatio Gates. This group is now known as the Conway Cabal, but ultimately the cooler voices prevailed. Washington himself reassured the cabal that he had no imperial aims: "Whenever the public gets dissatisfied with my service...I shall quit the helm...and retire to a private life."

Chapter Forty-Two:
Political Victories Roll In as the Military Fighting Pauses

This winter brought a long lull in hostilities, with neither the Americans nor the British engaging in serious offensive operations from January to May. Except for Benedict Arnold's victory over the British at Ridgefield, Connecticut on April 27, 1777, all was quiet. King George III took the opportunity to ride once again in splendor from his palace to Westminster, where he once again addressed the opening of Parliament on the ever-distressing war in America:

Nothing could have afforded me so much satisfaction as to have been able to inform you...that my unhappy people [in the American colonies], recovered from their delusion, had delivered themselves from the oppression of their leaders and returned to their duty. But so daring and desperate is the spirit of those leaders, whose object has always been dominion and power, that they have now openly renounced all allegiance to the Crown, and all political connection with this country...and have presumed to set up their rebellious confederacies for independent states. If their treason be suffered to take root, much mischief must grow from it.

Despite the tough talk from King George III and the threat of yet more fresh and eager British reinforcements, a major breakthrough took place in the Americans' favor. The French government had been closely observing the British-American conflict. Always looking for ways to weaken its major rival on the international stage, and keen on avenging its stinging defeat during the French and Indian War, the French government was impressed by the Continental Army's ability to not just fight but even *capture* thousands of British regulars after the Battle of Saratoga.

The French were impressed enough to formally enter the war in support of Congress. Benjamin Franklin came to Paris, where he negotiated a permanent military alliance early in 1778. France became the first country to recognize the United States. Though France had set up a major aid program to the American cause in 1776, to which the Spanish added some secret funds, 1778's massively increased French support would prove to be vital in maintaining the tired and distraught Continental Army. This American-French alliance startled the more liberal members of Parliament. William Pitt urged his fellow legislators to end the war in America and unite with the United States against France.

Chapter Forty-Three:
France Joins the War Effort

Pitt's words proved to be unpersuasive, yet prophetic: within just a few years, Napoleon Bonaparte would take power in France and go on to conquer nearly all of Europe, from Spain to Russia. Not long after the French entrance into the war, Spain would join in on America's side in 1779, and the Dutch would join in 1780. The emergence of American allies sent shockwaves through Great Britain. Not only did this foreign intervention turn a regional conflict into a world war, but it also revealed a profound weakness in its fiscal-military empire – namely, the fact that Great Britain stood alone against a coalition of great powers with no allies, and depended on extended and vulnerable lines to hold its empire together. These countries provided not only moral support and military aid to the American cause, but also lent their well-established navies in an Atlantic blockade, which seriously interfered with Great Britain's main advantage over the patriots – her naval fleet.

Within months, the American allies would also create new theatres in the conflict. Thousands of British forces in New England were forced to withdraw from continental

America and take up garrison in the Caribbean. British colonies in the Caribbean produced valuable sugar that France, Spain, and the Dutch were threatening to seize. This large-scale reorganization of forces brought the British commander in chief, Sir Henry Clinton, to evacuate Philadelphia for New York. Meanwhile, Spanish forces drove British forces out of Florida.

Chapter Forty-Four:
Molly Pitcher

Seeing his chance, Washington struck the retreating British forces in the Battle of Monmouth Court House. The Americans' fighting spirit proved that despite the horrors and enlistment crises they had experienced at Valley Forge, they were still an effective fighting force, and had somehow only grown more effective over the course of time. The temperature remain almost consistently above one hundred degrees throughout much of this battle, such that heat stroke likely claimed more lives than musket fire. Many women risked their lives to bring water to thirsty soldiers in the June heat, thus giving rise to the legend of "Molly Pitcher."

Molly Pitcher was a nickname given to women who fought on behalf of the Americans. The nickname likely began with Mary Ludwig Hays, a close friend of Washington's wife Martha. Mary often followed the soldiers into battle to give them water, and to splash their cannons with water in order to cool the cannons down. Overheated cannons would not fire and could even break, so this was a crucial element of support that every artilleryman looked forward to. During the Battle of Monmouth Court House, the incredible heat made Mary's assistance all the more crucial.

When her husband was carried off the battlefield, Mary took his place at the cannon – loading and unloading it, helping the soldiers fire it, then cooling it down. At one point, a British musket ball or cannonball flew between her legs, tearing off the bottom of her skirt. Mary is said to have looked at the stunned men around her and casually replied, "Well, that could have been worse," then went back to loading the cannon. Joseph Plumb Martin likely wrote of her when he wrote into his journal:

A woman whose husband belonged to the artillery and who was then attached to a piece in the engagement, attended with her husband at the piece the whole time. While in the act of reaching a cartridge and having one of her feet as far before the other as she could step, a cannon shot from the enemy passed directly between her legs without doing any other damage than carrying away all the lower part of her petticoat.

Looking at it with apparent unconcern, she observed that it was lucky it did not pass a little higher, for in that case it might have carried away something else, and continued her occupation.

This battle proved to become the final battle in northern New England, but the experienced British columns managed to avoid defeat and capture. They retreated to New York, and set up strong defensive positions that drew the war into a stalemate. All eyes now turned to the southern theater of the war effort.

Chapter Forty-Five:
The Northern Fighting Ends and the Southern Theater Opens Up

The British war effort saw another great shift in focus. If the north would have had the strongest support for the patriots' cause, then the south would have had the strongest support for the loyalist cause. The south was also home to more recent immigrants who may have preferred the stability of colony life under the Crown over the potential chaos of a revolution. Finally, the south was home to a large number of slaves who would have preferred to live as free men and women under British rule than as slaves under American rule.

(The British held back from arming slaves en mass, however, because Britain would not ban slavery until 1833, and any support for emancipation in the British Americas would have immediate repercussions in the British Caribbean and West Indies colonies, which had many slaves. Indeed, prior to the foreign intervention from Spain, France, and the Dutch, it was the Americans who repeatedly sought to create slave insurrections in these colonies).

The British estimates at the time were not far off. Historians today have reached a general consensus that while about half of the colonials supported the patriots' cause to at least some extent, about fifteen to twenty percent of colonials supported the British Crown. The rest of the population kept a low profile and tried to stay neutral. Quakers, for instance, were loudly neutral for religious reasons, though the "join or die" philosophy led many patriots to accuse them of being loyalists in all but name by not supporting the revolution.

Chapter Forty-Six:
The Meaning of "Patriot" Takes Shape

Most patriots were simple people who would not have been able to explain the Lockean ideas offered in the Declaration of Independence. Instead, most patriots would likely have stressed their feelings about their rights of being left alone, being treated fairly, and agreeing to their government's action. The violent British responses to pre-war colonial unrest, and especially the British use of military force and repression instead of reconciliation, helped convince many otherwise neutral people that the Crown had grown tyrannical and had become an enemy instead of a protector.

By contrast, loyalists were generally older and connected somehow to either the Church of England or British business, by way of merchant ties. Unlike the self-reliant farmers who were often patriots, the loyalists were often business whose livelihood depended on trade with Britain and/or some of its other colonial possessions. Naturally, British Americans in a position of power were also either loyalists, or too closely tied with the Crown to be trusted. Sadly, this split up many families. Even Benjamin

Franklin's own family was not spared the difficult question of loyalties, because his son William Franklin was a royal governor of the Province of New Jersey. The two men never spoke again.

But after the war, only a minority of the approximately half-million loyalists would decide or be forced to relocate (those who did relocate primarily went to Canada, with some going to Britain, Florida, or the West Indies). Most loyalists would be able to resume their normal pre-war lives. Some, like Samuel Seabury, would even become prominent American leaders.

Late in 1778, the British fired their first shot in this new campaign when they captured Savannah and seized control of Georgia's coastline. After the Continental Army mounted unsuccessful counter-attacks around Georgia, the British regulars went on to capture Charleston in 1780. British victory at the Battle of Camden ensured that the British would control the lion's share of South Carolina, as well as Georgia. The British secured their victories by creating a series of forts and encouraging the local residents to rise up in defense of the Crown.

In a turn for the worse, very few loyalists turned up to support the British cause. The British regulars continued upwards with their advance into North Carolina and Virginia, but they were overextended, tired, and weakened from constant fighting. Their entire strategy had depended on the idea that the south was the home of the loyalist cause, and that thousands of loyalists would replenish the British ranks. Instead, the opposite occurred: when the British forces marched up and left behind small garrisons in Georgia and South Carolina, the chaos of guerilla war broke out in both territories and ate away at much of the control that the British regulars had gained.

Chapter Forty-Seven:
The Southern Strategy Dries Up and Loses Steam

By 1781, the Crown's attempt to win the American Revolution by seizing the south had grown stale. The Second Continental Congress had finally ratified the Articles of Confederation, and now became the Congress of Confederation. The Congress of Confederation was the Americans' undisputed leader, and would oversee the rest of the war effort. Further, they had already appointed the man who is technically the first president of the United States, John Hanson of Maryland. Congress declared that the "president of the United States in Congress assembled" would take "precedence of all and every person in the United States."

George Washington himself wrote, "I congratulate your Excellency on your appointment to fill the most important seat in the United States." Under Hanson's leadership, the United States established its treasury department, adopted its seal (which is still in use today), and declared the fourth Thursday of every November as "a day of Thanksgiving."

After Hanson, six more presidents went on to lead the next six sessions of Congress, with each being referred to as "president" by the congress members and by Washington himself. (Legally, of course, Washington would become the first president under the U.S. Constitution; the previous seven presidents had led under the authority of the Articles of Confederation, which the Constitution replaced).

As for the war effort, the British regulars were now exhausted from nearly a decade of constant fighting in a foreign land. They were too few and far in between to capture and retain the incredible of land that they were tasked with occupying. The regulars were campaigning in Virginia when their commander in chief, Cornwallis, called for a momentary pause. The locals had come to be overwhelming, so Cornwallis called on the British fleet to rescue them from the hostile territory and angry farmers all around them.

Chapter Forty-Eight:
The Final Battle at Yorktown

Cornwallis agreed to meet the fleet at Yorktown, Virginia. They selected Yorktown because it struck them as hardly worth defending. There were just sixty private occupied houses and only a handful of public buildings in Yorktown. Further, whoever controlled the waters would control Yorktown, because it had the Atlantic on one side and a river on the other. Further, there were no woods or other natural obstacles that an advancing infantryman could hide under during an advance; thus, any attack would face severe losses.

The British fleet showed up as promised, but in an unexpected turn of events, a larger French fleet also showed up. They fought for control of the waters in the Battle of the Chesapeake, and the French emerged victorious. The British fleet retreated up north to New York, where it hoped to get reinforcements to bring to the south. However, that trapped Cornwallis at Yorktown. The Americans refused to advance, precisely because the lack of obstacles would doom an American advance to heavy casualties.

However, French control of the Atlantic angle and the river angle to Yorktown, as well as the constant pressure that the American positions were exerting, made the defense of Yorktown exceedingly difficult. And the same lack of obstacles preventing an American advance was now preventing a British advance from Yorktown. Despite his best efforts to await the reinforcements from up north, Cornwallis admitted that it would be impossible to fight off the combined French and Continental forces, then surrendered his army.

Chapter Forty-Nine:
"O' God, It Is All Over"

Washington and Cornwallis held talks to decide on the terms of surrender, then agreed that the formal ceremony of surrender would occur on October 19. As excited as he was to capture a major British force, Washington was careful not to make an overly vainglorious remarks or demands; such a display would only ensure that an outraged British public would send yet more British regulars to the British Americas. Instead, the ceremony was had at two o'clock in the afternoon, with American soldiers, French sailors, and British soldiers standing in grand detachments and holding their rifles proudly.

Washington and his French counterparts appeared, but Cornwallis decided not to show up. They proceeded with the surrender ceremony anyway, at the end of which they asked they British to lay down their rifles into a pre-marked pile. The British soldiers did so, but with such violence that their muskets were breaking upon hitting the ground. American officers stepped in to preserve the weapons, and the surrender – as well as the entire American Revolution along with it – had come to an end.

King George took the news without much concern, and was ready to fight on. However, Great Britain's populace had grown sick of the pointless and costly war effort, which had seen so many blunders, casualties, and was now dragging into its sixth year. Many members of the British public had also sympathized with the patriots' cause. Though this sympathy was largely erased after the attempted invasion of Canada, which was seen as an imperialistic instead of democratic attack, the public support for the war continued to reach newer and newer lows as British regulars failed to secure a decisive victory – month after month, year after year. Upon hearing the news a few weeks later, Lord Nord said exactly what was on his mind: "O' God, it is all over."

King George's support in the Parliament evaporated. He lost control of Parliament, and found himself unable to order any new major land offensives in North America – this, despite the fact that he had twenty-six thousand troops in New York and Savannah, as well as a powerful fleet. In addition, French ground and naval forces left North America in 1782, which meant that the Continental Army was on its own again. The treasury Congress had set up was well beyond empty, and the soldiers of the

Continental Army had not been paid in quite some time.

Officers seriously feared the possibility of mass desertion, a mutiny, or even a counter-revolution. Their fears turned true in 1783 with the Newburgh Conspiracy, which prompted Congress to promise a five-year bonus to all officers.

Section Five: 1781-1783, The Final Years and Aftermath

Chapter Fifty: The Pre-Negotiations Tension is Palpable

Washington, meanwhile, read every English newspaper that he could get his hands on. He was not aware of British intentions for continuing the war effort, and suspected that the British themselves did not know what to do at this point. Washington's letters at the time show how keenly interested he was in seeking information about the British enemy from their newspapers and defectors, to see if Great Britain would strain their resources further to fight the Europeans or the Irish. He certainly found it disturbing to read one day that Great Britain would grant concessions to the Irish, thus opening themselves to further on the American question. Just as the Yorktown surrender had come to an end, Washington was already asking the French admirals if they could stay a bit longer to support an American offensive into Charleston.

But the French sailed away to the British West Indies, revealing that seizing the West Indies was their true intention in entering the war, not helping the Americans take control of British America. The French fleet being "so close but so far" had been a recurring theme throughout the later phrases of the Revolution, with many officers grumbling and complaining about the lack of French support. Washington, however, thanked the French admirals for whatever support they did give, and even told historians to ascribe the victory at Yorktown to the French.

Washington continued to plan for campaigns in the absence of French naval support, just in case the British refused to discuss a peace treaty, or refused to recognize American independence as part of a peace treaty, or used peace negotiations as an excuse to prepare for their next ground offensive. Washington found during this time that he seemed to be the only one still thinking about war, while the rest of the colonies were dreaming of more peaceful days to come. He could only hope that their intuition was right.

Ultimately, the British launched no major offensives for the Continental Army to repel. And had the British launched an offensive, the soldiers of the Continental Army would likely have put aside their grievances, having come so far in the war effort and sacrificed too much to allow their war effort to crumble beneath the weight of some mundane internal squabbling. Instead, the British focused their next offensive on securing the best possible position for the peace negotiations in Paris. After the British caved in to the American demand that no negotiations would begin until Great Britain recognized American independence, all eyes turned to the peace conference that took place in Paris.

Chapter Fifty-One:
The Treaty of Paris

The Treaty of Paris was every bit as combative and hostile as the revolutionary war itself. The French delegation, shockingly enough, supported independence but refused to support any territorial gains. Under this position, the new United States of America would be confined to the area east of the Appalachian Mountains. Hoping to secure a better deal, the Americans decided to negotiate directly with the British. The British Prime Minister Lord Shelburne took this as a chance to do what William Pitt suggested, years ago, and turn the Americans into an ally against the French.

The British therefore offered a very generous deal: if the U.S. would agree to let British merchants and loyalists recover their property, then the U.S. and Great Britain would be at peace, and the U.S. could receive all of the land east of the Mississippi River, south of Canada, and north of Florida. Lord Shelburne hoped that a generous deal with the U.S. would not only ease the relationship between the U.S. and Great Britain, but also enable an enriched U.S. to rapidly grow and, once it abandoned its weak Articles of Confederation for the U.S.

Constitution, become a valuable ally and trading partner with Great Britain.

This gamble paid off handsomely, at least in the short run (American-English relations would sour again after 1800, ultimately leading to the War of 1812). American and British economies, which were both badly in need of resources to replenish their depleted treasuries, boomed after the American Revolution. Emotionally, it was difficult for the British to let go of so much, and just as difficult for the Americans to find themselves. Even the cool-headed, diplomatic George Washington later wrote that "From the former infatuation, duplicity, and perverse system of British Policy; I confess I am induced to doubt everything & to suspect everything" from the British. Trust was and continues to be an especially difficult thing to earn.

William Pitt would go on to become the new prime minister, signaling a bright future for American-British relations. Because of the strong cross-Atlantic relations, the loss of the American colonies did not mean an end to the British Empire. Great Britain's imperial ambitions merely went elsewhere, to Asia, the Pacific, and Africa, in what would become known as the Second British Empire. Washington, meanwhile, found himself on a letter-writing campaign, reminding Congress and the heads of the various new executive bodies of the promises given to the Continental Army soldiers and officers. The military men feared that Congress would forget its promises, and disband the military entirely without honoring the pay and land that had been promised. This would an affront not only to the soldiers themselves, but to the institution they had all been fighting for after all these years.

Chapter Fifty-Two:
The Post-War Continental Army and the Native Americans

In a less likely but still ominous turn of events, a congressional refusal to settle the soldiers' accounts might spark yet another revolution, with the soldiers marching on Congress and establishing the very kind of military order that they had all fought so long to repel. Such a struggle would surely "cast a shade over the glory which has been justly acquired; and tarnish the reputation of an Army which is celebrated thro' all Europe, for its fortitude and Patriotism." It is often forgotten that the Continental Army was for many years the only reliable, fully-functioning institution in colonialist politics. A lesser man than Washington could very easily have seized power after the war, and established himself as dictator. One of the many great legacies that George Washington would leave behind, then, is the legacy of civilian supremacy over even the most important military affairs.

Moreover, there was still one formidable enemy for army to fight. The backdoor, secret negotiations during the Treaty of Paris left out not only the French, but also Great Britain's long-time allies in the western North American hemisphere, namely the indigenous tribes. The quarter-million Native Americans living east of the Mississippi distrusted colonialists, and had spent the better part of the last few decades fighting against westward colonialist expansion. Further, many Native Americans tribes had lucrative trading relationships with British outposts, and were tempted by the Crown's offer to keep its colonies restricted to the coastline and east of the Appalachian Mountains.

Despite this, most Native American tribes did not directly participate in the war. Great Britain had been their enemy for too long; the Crown's sudden offers of friendship were obviously made in desperation. France had been their age-old friend, and France was a loyal friend – if France favored the Americans and hated the English, then perhaps it would be wiser to let the Americans and British fight out their differences on their own. Still, four Iroquois nations in New York and Pennsylvania were the tribes that actively participated in the war as British allies, generally by raiding American towns. Britain had no other major tribal allies in the upper Midwest.

Interestingly, the Iroquois of central and western New York supported the American cause, and most other tribes ultimately stayed out of the conflict – in part because they were still recovering from a massive outbreak of plague that decimated massive amounts of Native Americans, and in part out of fear of reprisals from whoever lost the war.

The Native Americans played no role in the Treaty of Paris and refused to recognize it. British financial support to the Native American tribes continued until 1795, when the Jay Treaty put an end to it. American settlers rushed into the new areas, rapidly creating the new state of Vermont, Kentucky, and Tennessee. This set up the American-indigenous conflict that would come to define much of American history, culture, and politics in the 18th and 19th centuries. As for the Cherokee and other Indian raids that took place in the south, particularly in South Carolina, it is worth remembering the historical context that in the decades between Columbus discovering America for the Europeans and the Mayflower's landing at Plymouth Rock, one of the most devastating plagues in history had decimated ninety-six percent of the Indians in Massachusetts, and a great deal of the Indian population throughout North America. If Native Americans were not keen on fighting, the fact that they were still recovering from a bona fide apocalypse may explain why.

Native societies would go on to influence the American government in many positive ways. The most important way is often cited as the Iroquois Confederacy's direct influence on the U.S. Constitution, which would be drafted in the years immediately following the American Revolution. For instance, the Iroquois Great Law of Peace "includes 'freedom of speech, freedom of religion … separation of power in government and checks and balances." The Senate even passed a resolution acknowledging that "the confederation of the original thirteen colonies into one republic was influenced...by the Iroquois Confederacy, as were many of the democratic principles which were incorporated into the constitution itself."

Chapter Fifty-Three:
The Meaning of the United States of America

American leaders felt acutely aware of the fact that the United States was the first country of its kind, a republic bound to its republican values instead of to any mortal. With its three branches and checks-and-balances system meant to keep the three branches in constant competition, the American government bore no resemblance to Europe's kings and queens, Africa's tribes, or Asia's and South America's warlords. Every other country at that time functioned on a system of autocratic rule, with the Western nations still retaining a class of nobility, and other trappings of their feudal history.

By stark contrast, the United States had a short-term president who did not "rule," but merely "presided" over the country's affairs. This bore far more resemblance to the ancient world's Roman republic and Greek democracy. Indeed, the American leaders borrowed extensively from Greek and Roman influences in their attempt to make John Locke's dream a reality. President Washington, like the nation's other leaders and citizens, firmly believed that the American republic would have to serve a mission well beyond its borders, to benefit not only the American people, but also all of humanity.

References

Opening Scene

Abernethy, David (2000). The Dynamics of Global Dominance, European Overseas Empires 1415–1980. Yale University Press. ISBN 0-300-09314-4. Retrieved 22 December 2015.

Adams, C.F. (1850–56), The works of John Adams, vol. VIII, pp. 255–257, quoted in Ayling, p. 323 and Hibbert, p. 165.

Anthony, Pagden (2003). Peoples and Empires: A Short History of European Migration, Exploration, and Conquest, from Greece to the Present. Modern Library. p. 90.

Bernard Semmel, The Rise of Free Trade Imperialism (Cambridge University Press, 1970) ch 1.

Black, Jeremy (2006). George III: America's Last King. New Haven: Yale University Press.

Bullion, John L. (2004). "Augusta, princess of Wales (1719–1772)". Oxford Dictionary of National Biography. Oxford University

Press. doi:10.1093/ref:odnb/46829. Retrieved 17 December 2015.

Cannon, John (2004). "George III (1738–1820)". Oxford Dictionary of National Biography (Oxford University Press). Retrieved 5 January 2016.

Carretta, Vincent (1990). George III and the Satirists from Hogarth to Byron. Athens, Georgia: The University of Georgia Press.

Chris Cook & John Stevenson, British Historical Facts 1760–1830 (The Macmillan Press, 1980).

David Andress, The Savage Storm: Britain on the Brink in the Age of Napoleon (2012).

Deryck Schreuder and Stuart Ward, eds., Australia's Empire (Oxford History of the British Empire Companion Series) (2010), ch 1.

Ferguson, Niall (2004). Empire, The rise and demise of the British world order and the lessons for global power. Basic Books.

Fred Anderson, The War That Made America: A Short History of the French and Indian War (2006).

"From 1707 until 1801 Great Britain was the official designation of the kingdoms of England and Scotland". The Standard Reference Work: For the Home, School and Library, Volume 3, Harold Melvin Stanford (1921).

Games, Alison (2002). Armitage, David; Braddick, Michael J, ed. The British Atlantic world, 1500–1800. Palgrave Macmillan. ISBN 0-333-96341-5.

Hecht, J. Jean (1966). "The Reign of George III in Recent Historiography". In: Elizabeth Chapin Furber, ed. Changing views on British history: essays on historical writing since 1939, pp. 206–234. Harvard University Press.

Hilton, Boyd. A Mad, Bad, and Dangerous People?: England 1783–1846 (New Oxford History of England) (2008).

Jenkins, Brian (2006). Irish Nationalism and the British State: From Repeal to Revolutionary Nationalism. Montreal & Kingston, ON: McGill-Queen's University Press. ISBN 9780773577756. Retrieved 9 January 2016.

John Ehrman, The Younger Pitt: The Consuming Struggle (1996), vol 3 cover 1797 to his death in 1806.

Kelso, Paul (6 March 2000). "The royal family and the public purse". The Guardian. Retrieved 9 January 2016.

Langford, Paul. A Polite and Commercial People: England 1727–1783 (New Oxford History of England) (1994).

Macalpine, Ida; Hunter, Richard A. (1991) [1969]. George III and the Mad-Business. Pimlico.

May, Thomas Erskine (1896). The Constitutional History of England Since the Accession of George the Third, 1760–1860 11th ed. London: Longmans, Green and Co.

O'Shaughnessy, Andrew Jackson (Spring 2004). "'If Others Will Not Be Active, I Must Drive': George III and the American Revolution". Early American Studies 2 (1): iii, 1–46.

Pinches, John Harvey; Pinches, Rosemary (1974). The Royal Heraldry of England. Heraldry Today. Slough,

Buckinghamshire: Hollen Street Press. pp. 215–216.

Röhl, John C. G.; Warren, Martin; Hunt, David (1998). Purple Secret: Genes, "Madness" and the Royal Houses of Europe. London: Bantam Press.

Royal Burials in the Chapel since 1805". St George's Chapel, Windsor Castle. Dean and Canons of Windsor. Retrieved 9 December 2015.

Smith, Robert A. (1984). "Reinterpreting the Reign of George III". In: Richard Schlatter, ed. Recent Views on British History: Essays on Historical Writing since 1966, pp. 197–254. Rutgers University Press.

Sondhaus, L. (2004). Navies in Modern World History. London: Reaktion Books. p. 9.

Speck, W.A. *Literature and Society in Eighteenth-Century England: Ideology, Politics and Culture, 1680–1820* (1998).

The Royal Household. "George III". Official website of the British Monarchy. Retrieved 10 January 2016.

Trevelyan, George (1912). George the Third and Charles Fox: The Concluding Part of the American Revolution. New York: Longmans, Green.

V. E. Hartley Booth & Peter Sells, British extradition law and procedure: including extradition between the United Kingdom and foreign states, the Commonwealth and dependent countries and the Republic of Ireland (Alphen aan den Rijn: Sijthoff & Noordhoff, 1980; ISBN 978-90-286-0079-9), p. 5.

Warren, Martin; Hunt, David (1998). Purple Secret: Genes, "Madness" and the Royal Houses of Europe. London: Bantam Press.

Watson, J. Steven. *The Reign of George III, 1760–1815* (Oxford History of England) (1960).

Wheeler, H. F. B.; Broadley, A. M. (1908). Napoleon and the Invasion of England. Volume I. London: John Lane The Bodley Head.

William E. Burns, A Brief History of Great Britain, p. xxi.

William R. Nester, The Great Frontier War: Britain, France, and the Imperial Struggle for North America, 1607–1755 (Praeger, 2000) p, 54.

Williams, Basil. *The Whig Supremacy 1714–1760* (1939).

Section One: 1740s-1775, Sowing the Seeds of the Revolution

Adams, James Truslow. Revolutionary New England, 1691–1776 (1923).

Alexander Keyssar, The Right to Vote (2000) pp 5–8.

Anderson, Fred (1984). A People's Army: Massachusetts Soldiers & Society in the Seven Years War. Chapel Hill, NC: University of North Carolina Press. ISBN 978-0-8078-4576-9.

Anderson, Fred (2000). Crucible of War: The Seven Years' War and the Fate of Empire in British North America, 1754–1766. New York: Alfred A. Knopf. pp. 267–285. ISBN 0375406425.

Anderson, Fred (2000). Crucible of War: The Seven Years' War and the Fate of Empire in British North America, 1754-1766. New York: Knopf. ISBN 0-375-40642-5.

Anderson, Fred. "The Real First World War and the Making of America" American Heritage, November/December 2005.

Anderson, Fred. The War That Made America: A Short History of the French and Indian War (2006).

Ann M. Becker, "Smallpox in Washington's Army: Strategic Implications of the Disease During the American Revolutionary War, *The Journal of Military History,* Vol. 68 No. 2 (April 2004) 388.

Bosher, Kate (1907). "The First House of Burgesses". The North American Review. 184 (612): 733–39.

Boyer, Clark, Kett, Salisbury, Sitkoff and Woloch. The Enduring Vision: A History of the American People.

Chidsey, Donald Barr (1966). The Siege of Boston: An on-the-scene Account of the

Beginning of the American Revolution. New York: Crown. OCLC 890813.

Churchill's Wizards: The British Genius for Deception, 1914–1945 (Rankin, Nicholas). p. 454 (2008 paperback).

Cogliano, Francis D. (2008). Revolutionary America, 1763–1815: A Political History. London: Routledge. p. 32. ISBN 9780415964869.

Core, Earl L. (1984), "The Monongalia River," in: Bartlett, Richard A. (ed), Rolling Rivers: An Encyclopedia of America's Rivers. New York: McGraw-Hill. ISBN 0-07-003910-0. pp 149–52.

Department of the Army, Lineage and Honors, 116th Infantry. Reproduced in Sawicki, James A. Infantry Regiments of the US Army. Dumfries, VA: Wyvern Publications, 1981. ISBN 978-0-9602404-3-2.

Dinkin, Robert J. Voting in Provincial America: A Study of Elections in the Thirteen Colonies, 1689-1776 (1977).

Drake, Samuel Gardner. A Particular History of the Five Years French and Indian War in New England.

Ellis, Joseph J. (2004). His Excellency George Washington. New York: Vintage Books. ISBN 1-4000-3253-9.

Fisher, Sydney George (1908). The Struggle for American Independence. J.B. Lippincott Company.

Fletcher Melvin Green (1930). Constitutional Development in the South Atlantic States, 1776-1860: A Study in the Evolution of Democracy. U. of North Carolina press. pp. 21–22. ISBN 9781584779285.

Fowler, William M. (2005). Empires at War: The French and Indian War and the Struggle for North America, 1754-1763. New York: Walker. ISBN 0-8027-1411-0.

French, Allen (1926). A British Fusilier in Revolutionary Boston. Harvard University Press.

Frothingham, Jr, Richard (1903). History of the Siege of Boston and of the Battles of Lexington, Concord, and Bunker Hill. Little and Brown. OCLC 221368703.

Gipson, Lawrence. The British Empire Before the American Revolution (15 volumes, 1936–1970), Pulitzer Prize.

Gordon S. Wood, *The American Revolution, A History*. New York, Modern Library, 2002 ISBN 0-8129-7041-1, p.14.

Green, Fletcher Melvin (1930). Constitutional Development in the South Atlantic States, 1776-1860: A Study in the Evolution of Democracy. U. of North Carolina press. ISBN 9781584779285.

Horgan, Lucille E. (2002). Forged in War: The Continental Congress and the Origin of Military Supply and Acquisition Policy. Praeger Pub Text. ISBN 978-0-313-32161-0.

Horn, James (2006). A Land as God Made It: Jamestown and the Birth of America, New York: Basic Books. ISBN 0-465-03094-7. pp. 123–124.

Howard H. Peckham, Pontiac and the Indian Uprising (1947); Richard Middleton, Pontiac's War: Its Causes, Course, and Consequences (2007).

J. R. Pole, Political Representation in England and the Origins of the American Republic (London; Melbourne: Macmillan, 1966), 31,
http://www.questia.com/read/89805613.

J. R. Pole, Political Representation in England and the Origins of the American Republic (London; Melbourne: Macmillan, 1966), 31,
http://www.questia.com/read/89805613.

John Wade, "British History Chronologically Arranged, 2: Comprehending a Chamfied Analysis of Events and Occurencis in Church and State ... from the First Invasions by the Romans to A.d. 1847", p.46 [1].

Johnson, Allen. "The Passage of the Sugar Act". *The William and Mary Quarterly*. 16 (4): 507–14.

Journals of the Continental Congress, pp. 26-44.

Lawrence Henry Gipson, "The American revolution as an aftermath of the Great War for the Empire, 1754-1763." Political Science Quarterly (1950): 86-104.in JSTOR.

Lee, Wayne E. "Fortify, Fight, or Flee: Tuscarora and Cherokee Defensive Warfare and Military Culture Adaptation." Journal of Military History (2004) 68.3 pp: 713-770.

Lt. John Barker, The King's Own Regiment, "Diary of a British Soldier," *Atlantic Monthly,* April 1877, vol. 39.

"Maine Legal Holidays". Human Resources Policy and Practices Manual. Maine Bureau of Human Resources. Archived from the original on 21 February 2009. Retrieved 6 January 2016.

Martino-Trutor, Gina Michelle. "Her Extraordinary Sufferings and Services": Women and War in New England and New France, 1630-1763" PhD Dissertation, U of Minnesota, 2012.

Middleton, Richard, and Anne Lombard. Colonial America: A History to 1763 (4th ed. 2011).

Moore, Frank (1876). *The Diary of the Revolution: A Centennial Volume.* Hartford, CT: J.B. Burr Publishing.

Murrin, John M. "The French and Indian War, the American Revolution, and the

Counterfactual Hypothesis: Reflections on Lawrence Henry Gipson and John Shy." Reviews in American History 1#3 (1973): 307-318. in JSTOR.

Nester, William R (2000). The first global war: Britain, France, and the fate of North America, 1756–1775. Westport, CT: Praeger. ISBN 978-0-275-96771-0. OCLC 41468552.

Osgood, Herbert L. The American colonies in the eighteenth century (4 vols, 1924–25).

Parkman, Francis. Montcalm and Wolfe: The French and Indian War. Originally published 1884. New York: Da Capo, 1984. ISBN 0-306-81077-8.

Paul Revere, Letter to Jeremy Belknap, January, 1798, and Paul Revere, Deposition, April, 1775.

Peckham, Harry H. The Colonial Wars, 1689-1762.

Robert Beeton, Naval and Military Memoreess of Great Britain, from 1727 to 1783, London: shortman, Hurst, Rees and Orme, 1804, vol. 6, pp. 203-206.

Rothbard, Murray (1975). *The Stamp Act Congress*. NY: Arlington House.

Salmon, Emily J. and Campbell, Jr., Edward D. C., editors, *The Hornbook of Virginia History*. Richmond, Virginia: The Library of Virginia, 1994.

Sawicki, James A. (1981). Infantry Regiments of the US Army. Dumfries, VA: Wyvern Publications. ISBN 978-0-9602404-3-2.

Smith, Justin H (1903). Arnold's March from Cambridge to Quebec. New York: G. P. Putnam's Sons.

Stanard, William G. and Mary Newton Stanard. The Virginia Colonial Register. Albany, NY: Joel Munsell's Sons Publishers, 1902. OCLC 253261475, Retrieved 3 January 2016. p. 52.

Taylor, Alan. American colonies (2002), 526 pages.

"The Battle of the Monongahela". World Digital Library. 1755. Retrieved 4 January 2016.

The First Colonial Soldiers: A Survey of British overseas territories and their garrisons, 1650 - 1714. Volume 2: The Americas and the Caribbean (Eindhoven: Drenth Publishing, 2015).

Thomas Cooper and David James McCord, eds. The Statutes at Large of South Carolina: Acts, 1685–1716 (1837) p 688.

U.S. Bureau of the Census, A century of population growth from the first census of the United States to the twelfth, 1790–1900 (1909) p 9.

"Unit Histories: From Portsmouth Harbor to the Persian Gulf," New Hampshire Army National Guard Pamphlet 600-82-3.

Verner W. Crane, "The Southern Frontier in Queen Anne's War," American Historical Review Vol. 24, No. 3 (Apr., 1919), pp. 379–395 JSTOR 1835775.

Woody Holton, "The Ohio Indians and the coming of the American revolution in Virginia," Journal of Southern History, (1994) 60#3 pp 453–78.

Zeisberger, David, David Zeisberger's History of the Northern American Indians in 18th Century Ohio, New York and Pennsylvania, pg 43; Wennawoods Publishing, 1999, ISBN 1-889037-17-6.

Zelner, Kyle F. A Rabble in Arms: Massachusetts Towns and Militiamen during King Philip's War (New York: New York University Press, 2009).

Section Two: 1775-1776, A String of American Victories From Boston to New York City

Ashworth, John, "The Jeffersonians: Classical Republicans or Liberal Capitalists?" *Journal of American Studies* 18 (1984), p 428-430.

Banner, James M. (1970). *To the Hartford Convention: The Federalists and the Origins of Party Politics in Massachusetts, 1789–1815.*

Bemis, Samuel F. (1923). Jay's Treaty: A Study in Commerce and Diplomacy. New York City: The Macmillan Company. ISBN 0-8371-8133-X.

Beyond the Founders: New Approaches to the Political History of the Early American Republic.

Bird, Harrison (1963). "March To Saratoga General Burgoyne And The American Campaign 1777". New York Oxford University Press.

Black, Jeremy (2004). Parliament and Foreign Policy in the Eighteenth Century. England: Cambridge University Press. p. 21. ISBN 0-521-83331-0.

Bumgarner, John R. (1994). The Health of the Presidents: The 41 United States Presidents Through 1993 from a Physician's Point of View. Jefferson, N.C: McFarland & Co. ISBN 0-89950-956-8.

Chambers, William Nisbet. *Political Parties in a New Nation: The American Experience, 1776–1809* (1963).

Charles O. Lerche, Jr., "Congressional Interpretations of the Guarantee of a Republican Form of Government during Reconstruction," Journal of Southern History (1949), 15:192-211 in JSTOR.

Colbourn, Trevor. *The Lamp of Experience: Whig History and the Intellectual Origins of the American Revolution* (1965).

Currie, James T., *The Constitution in Congress: The Federalist Period, 1789–1801,* (1997); *The Constitution in Congress: The Jeffersonians, 1801–1829,* U. of Chicago Press, 2001.

David Tucker, *Enlightened republicanism: a study of Jefferson's Notes on the State if Virginia* (2008) p. 109.

Du Bois, William Edward Burghardt (1904). The suppression of the African slave-trade to the United States of America. Longmans, Green and Co.

Elkins, Stanley M.; McKitrick, Eric L. (1993). The Age of Federalism. McEwan, Barbara (1991).

Edmund Morgan, The Birth of the Republic: 1763-1789 (1956) pp 82-83.

Ellis, Joseph J. (1996). American Sphinx: The Character of Thomas Jefferson. Alfred A. Knopf. ISBN 978-0-679-44490-9.

Ellis, Joseph J. (2004). His Excellency: George Washington. New York: Alfred A. Knopf. ISBN 1-4000-4031-0.

Espinosa, Gastón (2009). Religion and the American Presidency: George Washington to George W. Bush with Commentary and Primary Sources. New York: Columbia University Press. ISBN 978-0-231-14332-5.

Ferling, John E. (2000). Setting the World Ablaze: Washington, Adams, Jefferson, and the American Revolution. New York: Oxford University Press. ISBN 0-19-513409-5.

Fleming, Thomas. Washington's Secret War: The Hidden History of Valley Forge. 2005. ISBN 0060829621.

Freedman, Russell (2008). Washington at Valley Forge. New York: Holiday House. p. 44.

Hans Sperber and Travis Trittschuh, *American Political Terms: An Historical Dictionary* (1962) p 150.

Hartog, Jonathan J. Den. *Patriotism and Piety: Federalist Politics and Religious Struggle in the New American Nation* (University of Virginia Press; 2015).

Hellenbrand, Harold (1990). The Unfinished Revolution: Education and Politics in the

Thought of Thomas Jefferson. Associated University Presse. ISBN 978-0-87413-370-7.

Hicks, Paul. The Spymaster and the Author. The Rye Record, December 7, 2014.

Higginbotham, Don, ed. (2001). George Washington Reconsidered. Charlottesville: University Press of Virginia. ISBN 0-8139-2005-1.

Irvin, Benjamin H., *Clothed in Robes of Sovereignty: The Continental Congress and the People Out of Doors*, Oxford University Press, 2011, p. 5.

Jensen, Merrill (1948). The Articles of Confederation: An Interpretation of the Social-Constitutional History of the American Revolution, 1774–1781. Madison: University of Wisconsin Press. OCLC 498124.

Jensen, Merrill. *The Articles of Confederation: An Interpretation of the Social-Constitutional History of the American Revolution, 1774–1781* (1959).

Jillson, Calvin, and Wilson, Rick, Congressional dynamics: structure, coordination, and choice in the first American Congress, 1774–1789, Stanford University Press, 1994, p. 5.

Joyce Appleby, *Capitalism and a New Social Order: The Republican Vision of the 1790s*, 1984.

Ketchum, Richard (1999). The Winter Soldiers: The Battles for Trenton and Princeton. Holt Paperbacks; 1st Owl books ed edition. ISBN 0-8050-6098-7.

Ketchum, Richard M (1997). Saratoga: Turning Point of America's Revolutionary War. New York: Henry Holt. ISBN 978-0-8050-6123-9. OCLC 41397623. (Paperback ISBN 0-8050-6123-1).

Klein, Milton, *et al.*, eds., *The Republican Synthesis Revisited* (1992).

Kloppenberg, James T. *The Virtues of Liberalism* (1998).

Kyle G. Volk, "The Perils of 'Pure Democracy': Minority Rights, Liquor Politics, and Popular Sovereignty in Antebellum America," Journal of the Early Republic Volume 29, Number 4, Winter 2009 doi:10.1353/jer.0.0113.

Volk, Kyle G. (2014). Moral Minorities and the Making of American Democracy. New York: Oxford University Press.

Laboratory of Justice, The Supreme Court's 200 Year Struggle to Integrate Science and the Law, by David L. Faigman, First edition, 2004, p. 34; Smith, Republic of Letters, 15, 501.

Landa M. Freeman, Louise V. North, and Janet M. Wedge, eds. Selected Letters of John Jay and Sarah Livingston Jay: Correspondence by or to the First Chief Justice of the United States and His Wife (2005)

Lockhart, Paul Douglas (2008). The Drillmaster of Valley Forge — The Baron de Steuben and the Making of the American Army and moving forward with the revolution". HarperCollins (New York). ISBN 0-06-145163-0.

McCormick, Richard P., "Ambiguous Authority: The Ordinances of the Confederation Congress, 1781–1789", The American Journal of Legal History, Vol. 41, No. 4 (Oct., 1997), pp. 411–439, p. 438.

Merrill Jensen, "The American Revolution Revolution Within America", New York University Press, 1974, pp. 213-214.

Mitchell, Broadus (1962). *Alexander Hamilton: The National Adventure, 1788–1804.* McMillan.

Morgan, Edmund (1956). *The Birth of the Republic: 1763–1789.* pp. 82–83.

Morison, Samuel Eliot. Harrison Gray Otis, 1765-1848: The Urbane Federalist (1969)Jeffrey L. Pasley, et al. eds., ed. (2004).

Morris, Richard B. ed. John Jay: The Making of a Revolutionary; Unpublished Papers, 1745–1780 1975.

Morris, Richard. John Jay: The Winning of the Peace. New York: Harper & Row Publishers, 1980.

Olive Baldwin and Thelma Wilson. "John Burgoyne". In Macy, Laura. Grove Music Online. Oxford Music Online. Oxford University Press.

Olsen, Neil, *Pursuing Happiness: the Organizational Culture of the Continental*

Congress, Nonagram Publications, 2013, pp. 114–114.

Pancake, John (1985). This Destructive War. University of Alabama Press. ISBN 0-8173-0191-7.

Parry, Jay A.; Allison, Andrew M. (1991). The Real George Washington: The True Story of America's Most Indispensable Man. United States: National Center for Constitutional Studies. ISBN 978-0-88080-014-3.

Paul A. Rahe, Republics Ancient and Modern: Classical Republicanism and the American Revolution. Volume: 2 (1994) P. 23.

Phillips, Julieanne (1997). "Northwest Ordinance (1787)". In Rodriguez, Junius. The Historical Encyclopedia of World Slavery. ABC-CLIO. pp. 473–74.

"Portrait Gallery". The Historical Society of the Courts of the State of New York. New York State Unified Court System. Retrieved 4 January 2016.

Purcell, L. Edward. *Who Was Who in the American Revolution*. New York: Facts on File, 1993.

Rakove, Jack N. The Beginnings of National Politics: An Interpretive History of the Continental Congress, Knopf, 1979.

Randolph quoted in Banning (1978) p. 262. See Lawrence D. Cress, "Republican Liberty and National Security: American Military Policy as an Ideological Problem, 1783 to 1789." *William and Mary Quarterly* (1981) 38(1): 73–96. ISSN 0043-5597.

Resch, John P., ed. *Americans at War: Society, Culture and the Homefront* vol 1 (2005).

Richard Buel, *Securing the Revolution: Ideology in American Politics, 1789–1815* (1972).

Robert E. Shalhope, "Toward a Republican Synthesis: The Emergence of an Understanding of Republicanism in American Historiography," William and Mary Quarterly, 29 (January 1972), 49–80.

Roger G. Kennedy, Burr, Hamilton, and Jefferson: A Study in Character (2000) p. 92.

Scheer, George (1987). Rebels and Redcoats. Da Capo Press. ISBN 0-306-80307-0.

Sharp, James Rogers (1993). *American Politics in the Early Republic: The New Nation in Crisis*. Yale University Press.

Smelser, "The Jacobin Phrenzy: Federalism and the Menace of Liberty, Equality and Fraternity," *Review of Politics* 13 (1951) 457–82.

The Battle of Saratoga - A Major Turning Point of The Revolutionary War". Saratoga.com. Retrieved 29 December 2015.

Thomas Jefferson, Farmer. McFarland. ISBN 978-0-89950-633-3.

Thomson, Peter. *The Cambridge Introduction to English Theatre, 1660-1900*. Cambridge University Press, 2006.

Todd Estes, "Shaping the Politics of Public Opinion: Federalists and the Jay Treaty Debate". Journal of the Early Republic (2000) 20(3): 393–422. ISSN 0275-1275; online at JSTOR.

Trussell Jr., John B. B. (1976). Birthplace of an Army: A Study of the Valley Forge

Encampment. Harrisburg, PA: Pennsylvania Historical and Museum Commission. p. 109. ISBN 0-911124-87-X.

Unger, Harlow Giles (2013). "Mr. President" George Washington and the Making of the Nation's Highest Office. Boston: Da Capo Press, A Member of the Perseus Book Group. ISBN 978-0-306-82241-4.

Wiencek, Henry (2003). An Imperfect God: George Washington, His Slaves, and the Creation of America. New York: Farrar, Straus and Giroux. ISBN 0-374-17526-8.

William Alexander Robinson, "The Washington Benevolent Society in New England: a phase of politics during the War of 1812", *Proceedings of the Massachusetts Historical Society* 1916) vol 49 pp 274ff.

Wood, W.J Henry (2003). Battles Of The Revolutionary War. Da Capo Press. ISBN 0-306-81329-7.

Yarbrough, Jean M.; Jefferson, Thomas (2006). The Essential Jefferson. Hackett Publishing. ISBN 978-1-60384-378-2.

Zagari, Rosemarie. "Morals, Manners, and the Republican Mother," American Quarterly

Vol. 44, No. 2 (June 1992), pp. 192–215 in JSTOR.

Section Three: 1776-1777, American Victories Give Way to the British Empire's Might

Bailyn, Bernard, ed. (1993). The Debate on the Constitution: Federalist and Antifederalist Speeches, Articles, and Letters During the Struggle for Ratification. Part One: September 1787 to February 1788. The Library of America.

Bailyn, Bernard. The Ideological Origins of the American Revolution. Enlarged edition. Originally published 1967. Harvard University Press, 1992. ISBN 0-674-44302-0.

Barratt, Carrie Rebora (Fall 2011). "*Washington Crossing the Delaware* and the Metropolitan Museum". *The Metropolitan Museum of Art Bulletin*: pp. 5–19.

Bemis, Samuel Flagg. *John Quincy Adams and the Foundations of American Foreign Policy* (1949).

Bird, Harrison (1963). "March To Saratoga General Burgoyne And The American Campaign 1777". New York Oxford University Press.

Brookhiser, Richard (2011) *James Madison*. Basic Books.

Brooks, Noah (1900). Henry Knox, a Soldier of the Revolution: Major-general in the Continental Army, Washington's Chief of Artillery, First Secretary of War Under the Constitution, Founder of the Society of the Cincinnati; 1750–1806. New York: G.P. Putnam's Sons. OCLC 77547631.

Brutus (1787) "To the Citizens of the State of New York". In *The Complete Anti-Federalist, Volume 1* (2008). Ed. Herbert J. Storing. University of Chicago Press.

Burnett, Edmund Cody (1941). The Continental Congress: A Definitive History of the Continental Congress From Its Inception in 1774 to March 1789.

Calderhead, William L. "British Naval Failure at Long Island: A Lost Opportunity in the American Revolution," *New York History,* July 1976, Vol. 57 Issue 3, pp 321–338.

Chadwick, Bruce (2005). George Washington's War. Sourcebooks, Inc. ISBN 978-1-4022-2610-6.

Colonel David Humphreys, Aide De Camp to Gen. Washington, *The Life and Heroic Exploits of Israel Putnam, Major-General in the Revolutionary War,* Hartford: Silas Andrus and Son, 1847, p. 68.

Countryman, Edward. "The Uses of Capital in Revolutionary America: The Case of the New York Loyalist Merchants," William and Mary Quarterly, 49#1 (1992), pp. 3–28 in JSTOR.

David Syrett (June 15, 2005). Admiral Lord Howe. Naval Institute Press. p. 61. ISBN 978-1-59114-006-1.

Eaton, Cyrus (1865). History of Thomaston, Rockland and South Thomaston, Maine. Thomaston Historical Society I (Reprinted by Courier-Gazette, Inc. 1972 ed.). Hallowell, Masters, Smith & Co.

Fritz, Christian G. (2008). American Sovereigns: The People and America's Constitutional Tradition Before the Civil War. Cambridge University Press.

Goodfriend, Joyce D. Before the Melting Pot: Society and Culture in Colonial New York City, 1664-1730 (1994).

Griffiths, Thomas, *Maine Sources in The House of the Seven Gables* (Waterville, Maine, 1945).

Gruber, Ira (1972). *The Howe Brothers and the American Revolution.* New York: Atheneum Press.

Heidler, David S. "The Politics of National Aggression: Congress and the First Seminole War," *Journal of the Early Republic* 1993 13(4): 501–530.

Herbert E. Klingelhofer, "George Washington Discharges Monroe for Incompetence," *Manuscripts*, 1965 17(1): 26–34.

Holmes, David L. (Autumn 2003). "The Religion of James Monroe". Virginia Quarterly Review 79 (4): 589–606. Retrieved 9 January 2016.

Horgan, Lucille E. (2002). Forged in War: The Continental Congress and the Origin of Military Supply and Acquisition Policy. Praeger Pub Text. ISBN 978-0-313-32161-0.

Howe, Daniel Walker. *What Hath God Wrought: The Transformation of America, 1815–1848* (2007), Pulitzer Prize.

Jensen, Merrill (1959). The Articles of Confederation: An Interpretation of the Social-Constitutional History of the American Revolution, 1774–1781. University of Wisconsin Press. ISBN 978-0-299-00204-6.

Jillson, Calvin C. (2009). American Government: Political Development and Institutional Change (5th ed.). Taylor & Francis. ISBN 978-0-203-88702-8.

Jon Kukla, "A Spectrum of Sentiments: Virginia's Federalists, Antifederalists, and 'Federalists Who Are for Amendments,' 1787–1788," *Virginia Magazine of History and Biography,* 1988 96(3): 276–296.

Kochan, James (2001). *United States Army 1783–1811 (Men-at-Arms Series).* Osprey Military. pp. 13–15.

Larson, Edward J.; Winship, Michael P. (2005). The Constitutional Convention: A Narrative History from the Notes of

James Madison. New York: The Modern Library. ISBN 0-8129-7517-0.

Law, David S.; Versteeg, Mila (2012). "The Declining Influence of the United States Constitution". New York University Law Review 87 (3): 762–858.

Lengel, Edward G. General George Washington: A Military Life. New York: Random House, 2005. ISBN 1-4000-6081-8.

Levinson, Sanford (1987). "Pledging Faith in the Civil Religion; Or, Would You Sign the Constitution?". William & Mary Law Review 29 (113). Retrieved December 15, 2015.

Maier, Pauline (2010). Ratification: The People Debate the Constitution, 1787–1788. New York: Simon & Schuster. ISBN 978-0-684-86854-7.

Malcolm, George A. (1920). "Constitutional History of the Philippines". American Bar Association Journal 6.

Martin, James Kirby (1997). Benedict Arnold: Revolutionary Hero (An American Warrior Reconsidered). New York University Press. ISBN 0-8147-5560-7.

Martin, James Kirby, and Mark Edward Lender. A Respectable Army: The Military Origins of the Republic, 1763–1789. 2nd ed. Wheeling, Illinois: Harlan Davidson, 2006. ISBN 0-88295-239-0.

McCullough, David (2006), 1776, New York: Simon and Schuster Paperback, p. 12.

McDonald, Forrest (1985). Novus Ordo Seclorum: The Intellectual Origins of the Constitution. Lawrence: University Press of Kansas. ISBN 978-0-7006-0311-4.

McGuire, Thomas J. (2011). *Stop the Revolution: America in the Summer of Independence and the Conference for Peace.* Mechanicsburg, PA: Stackpole Books.

Merrill Jensen, *The New Nation: A History of the United States During the Confederation 1781–1789* (1950) pp 54–84.

Middleton, Simon. "The World Beyond the Workshop: Trading in New York's Artisan Economy, 1690-1740." New York History (2000): 381-416. Page Count: 37 in JSTOR.

Monk, Linda. "Amendment III". Annenberg Classroom. Leonore Annenberg Institute for Civics of the Annenberg Public Policy Center of the University of Pennsylvania. Retrieved 6 January 2016.

Morison, Samuel Eliot (1965). The Oxford History of the American People. Oxford: Oxford University Press. p. 312.

Morris, Ira K (1898). Morris's Memorial History of Staten Island, New York, Volume 1. Memorial Publishing Co.

Morris, Richard B. (1956). ""The Confederation Period and the American Historian"". "William and Mary Quarterly" 13 (2): 139–156. doi:10.2307/1920529. JSTOR 1920529.

Nelson, Paul David; Kohn, Richard H (January 1972). "Horatio Gates at Newburgh, 1783: A Misunderstood Role". The William and Mary Quarterly (Third Series, Volume 29, No. 1): 143–158. JSTOR 1921331.

Odesser-Torpey, Marilyn (2013). Insiders' Guide to Philadelphia & Pennsylvania Dutch Country. Morris Book Publishing, LLC. p. 26. Retrieved 10 December 2015.

President Washington's Indian War Wiley Sword, 1985, University of Oklahoma Press, pp. 148-150.

Proposed Amendments to the Articles of Confederation Journals of the Continental Congress, 1774–1789. Edited by Worthington C. Ford et al. 34 vols. Washington, D.C.: Government Printing Office, 1904–37. 31:494–98.

Qing Yu, Li (1988). "Dr. Sun Yat Sen and the U.S. Constitution". In Starr, Joseph Barton. *The United States Constitution: Its Birth, Growth, and Influence in Asia*. Hong Kong: Hong Kong University Press.

Rakove, Jack N. (1979). "The Beginnings of National Politics: An Interpretive History of the Continental Congress". New York: Knopf. ISBN 0-394-42370-4.

Rappleye, Charles (2010). Robert Morris: Financier of the American Revolution. New York: Simon and Schuster. ISBN 9781416570912. OCLC 535493123.

Richard H. Popkin, "Thomas Jefferson's Letter to Mordecai Noah," *American Book Collector* 1987 8(6): 9–11.

Robertson, David Brian (2013). *The Original Compromise: What the Constitutional Framers Were Really Thinking*. New York: Oxford University Press.

Ronald Hoffman and Peter J. Albert, eds., *The Transforming Hand of Revolution: Reconsidering the American Revolution as a Social Movement*, 258–85. Charlottesville: University Press of Virginia, 1995.

Royster, Charles. A Revolutionary People at War: The Continental Army and American Character, 1775–1783. Chapel Hill: University of North Carolina Press, 1979. ISBN 0-8078-1385-0.

Rubin Stuart, Nancy. Defiant brides: the untold story of two revolutionary-era women and the radical men they married, Boston: Beacon Press, 2013. ISBN 9780807001172.

Scherr, Arthur. "James Monroe on the Presidency and 'Foreign Influence;: from the Virginia Ratifying Convention (1788) to Jefferson's Election (1801)." *Mid-America* 2002 84(1–3): 145–206. ISSN 0026-2927.

Sidbury, James. Ploughshares into Swords: Race, Rebellion, and Identity in Gabriel's Virginia, 1730–1810, Cambridge, 1997, pp. 127–28.

Skeen, C. Edward; Kohn, Richard H (April 1974). "The Newburgh Conspiracy Reconsidered". *The William and Mary Quarterly* (Third Series, Volume 31, No. 2).

Stewart, David O. (2007). *The Summer of 1787*. Simon and Schuster.

Still, Bayrd, ed. Mirror for Gotham: New York as Seen by Contemporaries from Dutch Days to the Present (New York University Press, 1956).

Tilly, Charles (1992). *Coercion, Capital, and European States*. Cambridge: Blackwell.

United States Department of Labor and Commerce Bureau of the Census (1909). A Century of Population Growth: From the First Census of the United States to the Twelfth, 1790–1900. D.C.: Government Printing Office.

Ward, Harry (1965). The Department of War, 1781–1795. Pittsburgh, PA: University of

Pittsburgh Press. ISBN 978-0-8229-8375-0. OCLC 569079.

Ware, Susan (2000). Forgotten Heroes: Inspiring American Portraits from Our Leading Historians. Portland, OR: Simon and Schuster. ISBN 978-0-684-86872-1. OCLC 45179918.

Wells, William V. *The Life and Public Services of Samuel Adams: Being a Narrative of His Acts and Opinions, and of His Agency in Producing and Forwarding the American Revolution, with Extracts From His Correspondence, State Papers, and Political Essays.* 3 volumes. Boston: Little, Brown, 1865.

William L. Calderhead, "British Naval Failure at Long Island: A Lost Opportunity in the American Revolution," *New York History,* July 1976, Vol. 57 Issue 3, pp 321-338.

"Why the Articles of Confederation failed." Originalism and Discover the Founding Principles. discoveringthefoundingprinciples.com. Retrieved 5 January 2016.

Wood, Gordon S. (1972). *The Creation of the American Republic, 1776–1787.* Chapel

Hill: University of North Carolina Press. p. 359.

Wood, Gordon S. (2009). *Empire of Liberty: A History of the Early Republic, 1789–1815.* Oxford University Press.

Wright, Jr., Robert K.; MacGregor Jr., Morris J. "Resolutions of the Continental Congress Adopting the Continental Army and other Sources from the Revolution". Soldier-Statesmen of the Constitution. E302.5.W85 1987. Washington D.C: United States Army Center of Military History. CMH Pub 71-25.

Section Four: 1777-1781, Stalemate in the North and the Empire's Southern Campaign

Alden, John (1981). The South in the Revolution, 1763 to 1789. Baton Rouge, LA: Louisiana State University Press. ISBN 978-0-8071-0003-5. OCLC 245906364.

An Officer in the Late Army (1858). A Complete History of the Marquis de Lafayette: Major-General in the American Army in the War of the Revolution. J. & H. Miller.

Anderson, Troyer Steele. *The Command of the Howe Brothers During the American Revolution*. New York and London, 1936.

Atwood, Rodney (1980). *The Hessians: Mercenaries from Hessen-Kassel in American Revolution*. Cambridge University Press.

Auricchio, Laura. *The Marquis: Lafayette Reconsidered* (Vintage, 2014).

Bicheno, H: Rebels and Redcoats: The American Revolutionary War, London, 2003.

Boatner, Mark M. III (1994). Encyclopedia of the American Revolution. Mechanicsburg, Pa.: Stackpole Books. ISBN 0-8117-0578-1.

Butterfield, Wilshire. An Historical Account of the Expedition Against Sandusky

Cashin, Edward J. *William Bartram and the American Revolution on the Southern Frontier*. Columbia: University of South Carolina Press, 2000.

Chinard, Gilbert (June 1936). "Lafayette Comes to America by Louis Gottschalk". Journal of Modern History 8 (2): 218.

Clary, David (2007). Adopted Son: Washington, Lafayette, and the Friendship that Saved the Revolution. Bantam Books. ISBN 978-0-553-80435-5.

Collins (editor), Varnum Lansing (1968). *A Brief Narrative of the Ravages of the British and Hessians at Princeton in 1776-1777.* New York: The New York Times and Arno Press.

Cont'l Cong., Commissions for Generals Pomeroy, Montgomery, Wooster, Heath, Spencer, Thomas, Sullivan, and Greene, in 2 Journals of the Continental Congress, 1774-1789 103 (Library of Cong. eds., 1905).

Cont'l Cong., Instructions for General Washington, in 2 Journals of the Continental Congress, 1774-1789 100-1 (Library of Cong. eds., 1905).

Crawford et al. Indian Warfare in Western Pennsylvania and north west Virginia at the time of the American Revolution.

Crow, Jeffrey J. and Larry E. Tise, eds. *The Southern Experience in the American Revolution.* Chapel Hill: University of North Carolina Press, 1978.

Davis, Burke (2007). The Campaign that Won America. New York: HarperCollins. ISBN 978-0-8368-5393-3.

Ferling, John E (2007). Almost a miracle: the American victory in the War of Independence. New York: Oxford University Press US. ISBN 978-0-19-518121-0.

Fleming, Thomas (1973). The Forgotten Victory: The Battle for New Jersey – 1780. New York: Reader's Digest Press. ISBN 0-88349-003-X.

Gruber, *The Howe Brothers in the American Revolution* (1972), p. 183.

Harvey, R: *A Few Bloody Noses: The American War of Independence*, London, 2001.

Jeremy Black, *War for America: The Fight for Independence, 1775-1783* (1998) pp 117-121.

John E. Ferling, *The First of Men: A Life of George Washington* (2010) ch. 9

Kathleen McKenna (June 10, 2007). "On Bunker Hill, a boost in La Fayette profile". Boston Globe.

Kepner, F, "A British View of the Siege of Charleston, 1776", *The Journal of Southern History*, Vol. 11, No. 1. (Feb., 1945), p. 94.

Ketchum, Richard M (1997). *Saratoga: Turning Point of America's Revolutionary War*. New York: Henry Holt.

Ketchum, Richard M (2004). *Victory at Yorktown: the Campaign That Won the Revolution*. New York: Henry Holt.

"Lafayette: Citizen of Two Worlds". Cornell University Library. 2006.

Lefkowitz, Arthur S. *George Washington's Indispensable Men: The 32 Aides-de-Camp Who Helped Win the Revolution*. Stackpole Books, 2003.

Letter from Cornwallis to Clinton, August 6th 1780", Clinton Papers; Clements Library, University of Michigan.

Lowell, Edward J. (1884). *The Hessians and the other German Auxiliaries of Great Britain in the Revolutionary War*. New York: Harper Brothers Publishers.

Mark M. Boatner, *Encyclopedia of the American Revolution*. Third Edition. Stackpole Books. 1994.

Martin, David G. *The Philadelphia Campaign: June 1777–July 1778*. Conshohocken, PA: Combined Books, 1993.

Martin, James Kirby, and Mark Edward Lender. *A Respectable Army: The Military Origins of the Republic, 1763–1789*. 2nd ed. Wheeling, Illinois: Harlan Davidson, 2006.

McGuire, Thomas J. *The Philadelphia Campaign, Vol. I: Brandywine and the Fall of Philadelphia*. Mechanicsburg, PA: Stackpole Books, 2006.

McGuire, Thomas J., *The Philadelphia Campaign, Vol. II: Germantown and the Roads to Valley Forge*. Mechanicsburg, PA: Stackpole Books, 2007.

McNeill, J.R. (October 18, 2010). "Malarial mosquitoes helped defeat British in battle that ended Revolutionary War". The Washington Post.

Morrissey, Brendan (1997). Yorktown 1781: the World Turned Upside Down. London:

Osprey. ISBN 978-1-85532-688-0. OCLC 39028166.

Morrissey, Brendan (1997). Yorktown 1781: the World Turned Upside Down. London: Osprey Publishing. ISBN 978-1-85532-688-0.

Palmer, Dave Richard (2006). George Washington and Benedict Arnold: A Tale of Two Patriots. Regnery Publishing. ISBN 978-1-59698-020-4.

Payan, Gregory (2002). Marquis de Lafayette: French Hero of the American Revolution. The Rosen Publishing Group. ISBN 978-0-8239-5733-0.

Reynolds, Jr., William R. (2012). *Andrew Pickens: South Carolina Patriot in the Revolutionary War*. Jefferson NC: McFarland & Company, Inc.

Ritcheson, C.; "Loyalist Influence on British Policy Toward the United States After the American Revolution"; Eighteenth-Century Studies; Vol. 7, No. 1; Autumn, 1973; p. 6.

Royster, Charles. *A Revolutionary People at War: The Continental Army and*

American Character, 1775–1783. Chapel Hill: University of North Carolina Press, 1979.

Russell, David Lee; *The America Revolution in the Southern Colonies*; 2009.

Sawicki, James A. (1981). Infantry Regiments of the US Army. Dumfries, VA: Wyvern Publications. ISBN 978-0-9602404-3-2.

Scammel, Alexander. "Return of the kill'd, wounded, missing and deserted since the 6th instant: Head Quarters, near Short-Hills, June 20th 1780". George Washington Papers at the Library of Congress, 1741–1799.

Syrett, D: "The British Armed Forces in the American Revolutionary War: Publications, 1875-1998", *The Journal of Military History*, Vol. 63, No. 1. (January, 1999), pp. 147–164.

Tarleton; *A History of the Campaigns of 1780 and 1781 in the Southern Provinces of North America*; 1787.

The Siege of Charleston; Journal of Captain Peter Russell, December 25, 1779, to May

2, 1780; *The American Historical Review*; Vol. 4, No. 3; Apr., 1899; p. 490.

Vowell, Sarah. *Lafayette in the Somewhat United States* (Riverhead, 2015).

Weigley, Russell (1991). The Age of Battles: The Quest For Decisive Warfare from Breitenfeld to Waterloo. Indiana University Press. ISBN 0-7126-5856-4.

Weintraub, S: *Iron Tears, Rebellion in America* 1775-1783, London, 2005.

Wickwire, Franklin and Mary (1970). Cornwallis: The American Adventure. Boston: Houghton Mifflin. OCLC 62690.

Wilson, David K (2005). *The Southern Strategy: Britain's Conquest of South Carolina and Georgia, 1775–1780*. Columbia, SC: University of South Carolina Press.

Wright, Jr., Robert K.; MacGregor Jr., Morris J. "Resolutions of the Continental Congress Adopting the Continental Army and other Sources from the Revolution". Soldier-Statesmen of the Constitution. E302.5.W85 1987. Washington D.C: United States Army Center of Military History. CMH Pub 71-25.

Section Five: 1781-1783, The Final Years and Aftermath

American Indian Sovereignty and the U.S. Supreme Court: The Masking of Justice, David E. Wilkins, University of Texas Press (1997), pp. 141–165, trade paperback, 421 pages, ISBN 978-0-292-79109-1.

Beckey, Fred (2003). Range of Glaciers: The Exploration and Survey of the Northern Cascade Range. Oregon Historical Society Press. pp. 101–114.

Brances G, Davenport and Charles O. Paullin, *European Treaties Bearing on the History of the United States and Its Dependencies* (1917) vol 1 p vii.

Bolme, Edward; Parks, Jim; Quintanar, Derek; Schumann, Mark; Cambias, James; Floch, Eric; Hyatt, Angela; Rosen, Barrie; Williams, Chris (1996). *Six-Guns & Sorcery*. Castle Falkenstein. Berkeley, CA: R. Talsorian Games.

Burr, Aaron. *Political Correspondence and Public Papers of Aaron Burr*. Mary-Jo

Kline and Joanne W. Ryan, eds. 2 vol. Princeton University Press, 1983. 1311 pp.

Cannon, P.F.; Hawksworth, D.L.; M.A., Sherwood-Pike (1985). *The British Ascomycotina. An Annotated Checklist.* Commonwealth Mycological Institute & British Mycological Society.

Carley, Kenneth (1961). The Sioux Uprising of 1862. Minnesota Historical Society. p. 65. Most of the thirty-nine were baptized, including Tatemima (or Round Wind), who was reprieved at the last minute.

Charles R. Ritcheson, "The Earl of Shelbourne and Peace with America, 1782–1783: Vision and Reality." *International History Review* (1983) 5#3 pp: 322–345.

Clark, Daniel. *Proofs of the Corruption of Gen. James Wilkinson, and of His Connexion With Aaron Burr: A Full Refutation of His Slanderous Allegations in Relation to ... of the Principal Witness Against Him* (1809). Reprinted by University Press of the Pacific, 2005.

Franklin, Benjamin. *The Papers of Benjamin Franklin: January 21 Through May 15,*

1783 (Vol. 39. Yale University Press, 2009).

George Clinton: Yeoman Politician of the New Republic by John P. Kaminski, New York State Commission on the Bicentennial of the United States Constitution, University of Wisconsin--Madison Center for the Study of the American Constitution (Rowman & Littlefield, 1993, ISBN 0-945612-17-6, ISBN 978-0-945612-17-9, page 24).

Gordon S. Wood, "Federalists on Broadway' *New York Review* (Jan 14. 2016).

Graebner, Norman A., Richard Dean Burns, and Joseph M. Siracusa. *Foreign affairs and the founding fathers: from Confederation to constitution, 1776–1787* (ABC-CLIO, 2011), pp. 199.

Kaminski, John P. *George Clinton: Yeoman Politician of the New Republic.* Madison House, 1993.

Kaminski, John P., "Clinton, George", The Encyclopedia of New York State, (Peter Eisenstadt, ed.), Syracuse: Syracuse University Press, 2005.

Kaplan, Lawrence S. "The Treaty of Paris, 1783: A Historiographical Challenge," *International History Review,* Sept 1983, Vol. 5 Issue 3, pp 431–442.

Kaplan, Lawrence S. "The Treaty of Paris, 1783: A Historiographical Challenge," *International History Review,* Sept 1983, Vol. 5 Issue 3, pp 431–442.

Kip, Lawrence (1859). *Army life on the Pacific: a journal of the expedition against the northern Indians, the tribes of the Cour d'Alenes, Spokans, and Pelouzes, in the summer of 1858.* Redfield.

Larson, Edward J. *A Magnificent Catastrophe: The Tumultuous Election of 1800, America's First Presidential Campaign.* New York: Free Press, 2007.

Life of George Bent: Written From His Letters, by George E. Hyde, edited by Savoie Lottinville, University of Oklahoma Press (1968), pp. 148–163, hardcover, 390 pages; trade paperback, 280 pages (March 1983).

Life of George Bent: Written From His Letters, by George E. Hyde, edited by Savoie Lottinville, University of Oklahoma Press

(1968), pp. 201–207, 212–222, hardcover, 390 pages; trade paperback, 280 pages (March 1983).

Lomask, Milton (1982). *Aaron Burr: The Conspiracy and Years of Exile, 1805–1836*. Aaron Burr **2**. New York: Farrar, Straus and Giroux.

Merrell, James H. (1989). "Some Thoughts on Colonial Historians and American Indians". *William and Mary Quarterly* 46 (1): 94–119.

Michno, F. Gregory (2009). *Encyclopedia of Indian wars: Western battles and skirmishes 1850–1890*. Missoula, Montana: Mountain Press Publishing Company.

Morris, Richard B. *The Peacemakers; the Great Powers and American Independence* (1965).

Quote from Thomas Paterson, J. Garry Clifford and Shane J. Maddock, *American foreign relations: A history, to 1920* (2009) vol 1 p 20.

Raphael, Ray. *A People's History of the American Revolution: How Common*

People Shaped the Fight for Independence. New York: The New Press, 2001.

Stewart, David O. (2007). *The Summer of 1787*. Simon and Schuster.

Smith, Sherry L (1998). "Lost soldiers: Researching the Army in the American West". *Western Historical Quarterly* 29 (2): 149–63.

"The Settler's War" of *The Battle of Beecher Island and the Indian War of 1867–1869*, by John H. Monnett, University Press of Colorado (1992), pp. 55–73, Chapter 3.

Thornton, Russell. *American Indian Holocaust and Survival: A Population History Since 1492*. Oklahoma City: University of Oklahoma Press, 1987.

Tucker, Spencer, ed. *The Encyclopedia of North American Indian Wars, 1607-1890: A Political, Social, and Military History* (3 vol 2012).

Van Ness, William Peter. *An Examination of the Various Charges Exhibited Against Aaron Burr, Vice-President of the United States: and a Development of the*

Characters and Views of His Political Opponents. (1803).

Vail, Philip. *The Great American Rascal: The Turbulent Life of Aaron Burr* (1973).

Weir, William (2003). *Written with Lead: America's Most Famous and Notorious Gunfights from the Revolutionary War to Today.*

Wiley Sword, *President Washington's Indian War: The Struggle for the Old Northwest, 1790-1795* (University of Oklahoma Press, 1985).

Wood, Gordon S. 2006 Revolutionary Characters. New York: Penguin.

52527030R00127

Made in the USA
Lexington, KY
01 June 2016